Mark Zupo

Mark Zupo

Mark Zupo

You Deserve to be Rich

The Secrets to Creating Your Destiny on Demand!

7-Level Success™ Series

By

Mark Zupo

Zupo, Mark

You Deserve to be Rich

The Secrets to Creating Your Destiny on Demand!

Copyright © 2010 Mark Zupo. Mark Zupo International, LLC All right reserved. No part of this book may be used or reproduced in any form without the prior written permission of the Author and Publisher. Printed in the United States of America.

ISBN-13: 978-0983994572 (Mark Zupo)

ISBN-10: 0983994579

Library of Congress catalog Card #

Also available in Audio CD format

To order, contact:

www.MarkZupo.com

SlipperyRock Press Publishing™

You deserve to be RICH!

DEDICATION

Dedicated to my wife,
Kay Stonesifer Zupo (1943-2005),
for saving my life.
Without whose memory, love, strength, support
and cheerful heart I would be lost forever.

And to my Mother, my Daughter, Traci, my Brother
and Sister, Chris and Rene for their undying
support and love over the years.

I am forever grateful to you all.

And to my wife, Kathy, a tower of strength,
patience and support, who believed in me when
others failed me.

In your trust.

A note from Mark

First I would like to say thank you for your trust.

I know there is a world of options out there but you chose to read my book. That is a very humbling and special thing for me. I am an entrepreneur who has published books, created online home study courses, created digital information books, mentor, trained and presented at various seminars both in-person and online. For the past 24 years I have been actively involved with mentoring in the success-motivation industry.

As a thought-leader and business mentor I have worked with businesses and people all over the world. I have worked with educators, business owners, individuals, entrepreneurs, lawyers, consultants, coaches, trainers and more. As founder of the **7-Level Success Academy**® I have helped these same people achieve personal and business success, improvement to life and happiness.
Maybe I can help you too.

Acknowledgments

Most importantly, the first person to thank is my Mother. Expressing my gratitude to her would take this entire book and encompass every emotion known to man, so I will just offer the most sincere thanks a son can offer:

> ***"All that I am and all that I hope to be, I owe to my mother."***
> ***-Abraham Lincoln***

I would like to acknowledge all of the entrepreneurially- motivated people in the world, especially those who acted on their gut instincts, their visions of opportunity and their sense of independence. I would like to acknowledge anyone who ever had a brilliant idea or moment of inspiration when he thought could change the world. Those are the people who, because of their efforts to achieve more and succeed when the odds are against them, motivate me to success.

Each individual may or may not be proud of the part they played in my life experiences that have contributed to who and what I am today. Some people were instrumental to my failures and some influential to my successes. Either way, I am better man for it.

I am especially thankful for those people who denied me, stopped me, held me back, crushed my enthusiasm, said no, didn't care, cheated me, refused me, snubbed me, were resentful of me, were indignant, slighted me, and challenged me.

To them, thanks for nothing—and...
> ***thanks for everything!***

- Mark Zupo

"DISCOVER THE SECRET TO MAKE YOUR KNOWLEDGE SELL USING MY TIME-TESTED STRATEGIES!"
"Your life will never be the same once you know what to do, who to talk to, how to position yourself, how to attract more business, more money and more enjoyment out of life!"

You are just one step away from a dynamic and charged opportunity to JumpStart your success with *free* membership the

7-Level Success™ Series

Insider's Membership Club.

When you join the **7-Level Success™ Series Insider's Membership Club**, you'll get you own free copy of: **You Deserve to be Rich** which is jammed packed with tips to motivate and inspire you to greater success, bigger profits and a better life decisions! **Yours *FREE!***

Mark Zupo

You deserve to be RICH!

"My unique understanding of leadership is the value of human potential and entrepreneurial spirit which is reinventing the world of success"

Mark Zupo

Mark Zupo

Preface

Throughout my life, I've been passionate and impassioned to do more, be better and achieve everything I can. My role models have been all of the successful entrepreneurs, dreamers and inventors or thought leaders that found their success from their individual effort and experiences. I firmly believe that anyone can achieve anything if they want to enough and are willing to work for it.

As an entrepreneur for more than 40 years, I believe that my success comes from an absolute lust for learning and from working hard and smart helping other people more than helping myself. I will always be a student in one form or another. In fact, I believe that I am a leader by choice and design rather than by accidental need. You deserve the best and the most that life has to offer. Don't just ask for it, go after it as you seek to serve others to help them achieve their dreams too.

Mark Zupo

"A business that makes nothing but money is a poor business".
- Henry Ford

Mark Zupo, a serial entrepreneur and author of the new book "Mind Your Business."

Mark established his first company, MZI, Inc. when he was only twenty-one years old. Since then, he has created and actively invested in multiple start-ups and has become a self-made multimillionaire. After he sold his first franchise company 1987, the global recession took the company to the brink of failure resulting in a complete loss and near bankruptcy. Mark as CEO went "all in" betting his last dollar on its potential and turned the company around from the edge of failure to more than $2,000,000 a year in revenue in only 14 months winning the minds and hearts of his family and followers. Recently interviewed for Talk Radio, Mark talks about how he re-branded himself after losing it all, the issues with the public education system, personal success and more.

This transcribed commentary was first a radio interview focusing on Mark's triumphs that detail how he overcame and championed over misfortune.

Mark says: "What I experienced isn't unique to anyone and might be diminished by people who have lost and suffered greater hardships than I. The difference is what road one takes after and how a person learns from their experiences."

"The choice to lead is a choice to serve"
- Mark Zupo

Thank you

You deserve to be RICH!

Table of Contents

Chapter 1	Dreams, Schemes and Designs
Chapter 2	Knowledge College
Chapter 3	"Brain-*wished*"
Chapter 4	A Method to the Madness
Chapter 5	Aptitude *vs.* Attitude
Chapter 6	"*Want-trepreneur*"
Chapter 7	Bear Poop and Panache
Chapter 8	Life, Liberty and the Pursuit
Chapter 9	The Big Picture
Chapter 10	Follow the Leader
Chapter 11	Passion Power, Persistence, Prosperity
Chapter 12	The Power to Prosper
Chapter 13	Intention, Attention, No Tension
Chapter 14	Destiny on Demand
Chapter 15	Life Clock ticking
Chapter 16	Get a Mentor

CHAPTER 1

DREAMS, SCHEMES AND DESIGNS

...EARNING INCOME FROM THE WORK YOU LOVE

We learn the skill to learn from school, we learn the skill of life from experience "

- Mark Zupo

"What is the Secret to Re-purposing Your Life?"

    I remember when I was working my way up in the first company that employed me, I used to have nightmares that one day they'd find out about me and my sorted history, call me into the office, and fire me. In the beginning I didn't talk much about what I'd been through. But eventually when I got to a point where I had established myself as a professional entrepreneur, I embraced my past, used it as part of my branding, and crossed over.

    Today, people want authenticity, honesty, trust and loyalty. The world is social and people know all about you, or can find out anything about you in a flash. It is nearly impossible to remove yourself from humanity today with the electronic messaging and databases that exist today. As I started showing my true identity as a leader and mentor, so did the rest of the world. One of the reasons I have known success as a fastest growing company in the industry today is because we share everything we know with anyone who asks for help. As a result of embracing authenticity, I have come to appreciate smaller successes and helping other people do the same.

We embrace our competitors and strive to affiliate ourselves with those who demonstrate honesty and willful concern for customer service and people's needs. Our customers know exactly who we are, what we do and how sincere we are when we do it. In my opinion, I believe that corporate America has a lesson to learn here.

Chances are you have spent life-time learning, studying, teaching and delivering information based on your experiences and expertise. Why haven't you profited from these passions while others have? If you're not sure of the steps necessary to find success in your passions, Mind Your Business will teach you. This book has been designed for those who want to change the direction of their lives and find success in their confidence, skills, background and passions.

It is no secret that people have talent and experience, background and expertise. They have energy and enthusiasm that until now has been devoted to making someone else rich. They have visions of their success but don't know how to take advantage of, benefit from and profit from - until now. This book provides you the opportunity to profit from what you have learned and experienced.

This book, **You Deserve to be Rich**, is for those who want to change the direction of their lives and find success in their confidence, skills, background and passions. Are you one of the aforementioned people? Have you spent lifetime learning, experiencing and believing you can be the very best at who you are and what you do?

I have always believed that your destiny is determined by your decisions. Ultimately, the path your life takes is directly proportional to the amount of education you have and the amount of labor you put into it. Some of the guidance you get is a direct link to your past experiences.

In this book, **You Deserve to be Rich**, you'll find the advice you need to form the business of "YOU!" You will find methods to help you grow as a business and profit from your expertise. This book will help you use your life's experience and passions to help other people do the same, while you earn a respectable fee for your services. After all, isn't that what a consultant does? He uses his knowledge to sell something.

How Can *This book* Help You Succeed?

Most people have a set of rules they follow based upon their experiences, education, wants, needs and desires. When you choose to follow a path you question, you usually come to an end that is predictable and distasteful; so follow the leadership of those who have succeeded before you by using their experiences, failures and successes as a guide for your opportunities. After all, we want to emulate someone we respect and admire, and most of us are willing to change our lives to accommodate that desire.

We want to emulate those we respect and admire, and many of us are willing to change our lives to do so. With this in mind, I implore you to consider the following questions.

√ What is one thing you would change about your life?

This question comes with the hope that when you adopt a change, you will be better off. It is laced with the indication that when change is adopted, you will have a better life: fame, fortune, admiration. You will be brought to the forefront of others' attention.

You should be warned, though, that change

also comes with risk, undefined hazards and ambiguous results. You will not be aware whether the risk is worth the reward until after you make the change, at which time it may be too late to reverse your decision.

This is like going back in time and changing whatever decisions may have been made along the way, thereby forever changing history. To the point of that scenario, your decisions and your motivation for success, freedom and wealth must be genuine and natural so you don't upset the balance of YOUR history.

√ What is stopping you from making that change?

Usually, we are held to our life's history by our decisions and opportunity. Notice I didn't say luck. I believe luck is the product of intuition, cognition, action and opportunity. I don't believe it is just happenstance. With that in mind, we have the ability to determine our course by some simple rules of intention.

We must:

- Achieve What You Believe because You Believe You Can Achieve.
- Know thyself and Thy business because You Are Your Business.
- Build a Legacy: It is Inheritable.

- Find the Message that Helps YOU Help Other People.

The power of intention is the driving force that determines your fate as a leader, an entrepreneur and a success in any endeavor in your life.

√ What do I know that will make me a living?

The most valuable resource you have is what you know! You have spent your lifetime gaining wisdom and knowledge that others have used for their benefit. Until now, you have made others rich; you have supported their successes by giving away valuable information you have accumulated. We both know you have a passion someone else would pay for. What you may not know is that your passions, your experiences, your education and your training have provided you knowledge so valuable that you could spend your entire life in luxury. You simply need to sell some portion of it to others who need that information. All you need is a way to present this knowledge to them! This is what I will teach you.

"You sometimes have to set unrealistic goals to achieve realistic results!"

Mark Zupo – 2009

This book is about know-how. Specifically, it is about your know-how. It is about the know-how you have spent a lifetime building while making mistakes, educating yourself to be the best you could be and experiencing all that life offers.

This book is about earning income from the work you love and the passions you have. It is about finding your personal place in the world; it is about using what you know and making a profit from it.

The idea for this book was drafted using a pen that I borrowed from a young lady who sat next to me on a flight from Los Angeles to Atlanta. Ashley S. and her husband Chris were returning from a vacation in Los Angeles, California, and didn't know who they were sitting next to or how it might change their lives. Although she did not know me, Ashley was kind enough to come to my aid; she lent me her pen to make notes for this book.

While talking to Ashley and her husband, I was overwhelmed by their commitment to each other and by Ashley's commitment to her business. Later, I couldn't help but reflect on how passionate Ashley was about her business, a business based on her own experiences, expertise and what she could do to help other people.

That is when it came to me - while sitting in

the airplane next to this bright, young couple. That is when I figured out that the value of a business isn't as much about the value of service as it is about the value of service you provide. It is about you.

As luck would have it, my best ideas generally come to me when I am least prepared. I do my best when I am captive to myself in a situation that doesn't allow me to escape myself, such as when I am traveling on an airplane. I think well when I'm trapped in my truck, a Ford 150 pick-up, or when I'm trapped on an airplane, generally one that I am not flying.

I firmly believe that my life is worth more than the life insurance that I carry against the loss of it. In fact, I believe in my heart that my life is worth more than all the gold in Fort Knox because my life is and will be as self-sustaining and as everlasting as I can make it. As long as my children continue to remember me, they will have the ability to capitalize on my life, just as Elvis's family has earned more on his fame than he ever did while he was alive.

I know that I am worth much more than anyone in corporate America is willing to pay me. That, my friends, is unacceptable. It is unacceptable for me, and it is unacceptable for you.

Your attitude about your self-worth is directly related to your income, and your perceived self-worth will fluctuate in parallel as your income wavers or teeters in either direction. Additionally, what you learned in school has had the greatest effect on what you believe your self-worth to be. This has been a great disservice to every American.

A true entrepreneur will find solutions where seemingly none exist, and he or she will triumph, no matter the risks or challenges. When we become educated to the value of what we desire, as opposed to the cost of the same, we can remove the blinders that keep us from success. In this book, you will find motivation, inspiration and guidance.

Take what you learn from this book and run with it, preferably to the bank. You will learn from experts who have built iconic lives out of a simple idea, a simple marketing plan and some luck and guts. Everyone has enough life experience to make a fortune, although most aren't aware of the power of their life experiences. You will discover that one's value is never as much as his worth until he learns how to market his life experience to the masses.

Is this you?

- ✓ **A highly motivated person?**
- ✓ **A self-starter?**
- ✓ **An independent thinker?**
- ✓ **A thought leader?**
- ✓ **Someone who makes things happen?**
- ✓ **Frustrated by a lack of opportunity?**

At this point, you know your success is dependent on you and you alone. You know there are barriers that get in the way but you have the energy to overcome them when opportunity knocks, right?

You know your motivation and inspiration comes from your successes! And you know your success comes from a well laid out plan and a well planned action to drive you to your dreams and achievements, but...

That's where I come in.

I am the mentor with the focus to detail and attention to clearly articulate the direction you need to focus on and the effort you need to give to get to your goals.

The question is...are you ready for an energetic and enthusiastic coach that will demand results and expect the kind of dedication that brings success?

Together we can draft your "Success Blueprint"... a "Road-Map" for the specific path for you to achieve and believe in your strengths and values.

The Plan:

- ✓ **Exercise Your Beliefs**
- ✓ **Focus on Your Dreams**
- ✓ **Define Your Goals**
- ✓ **Take Action**
- ✓ **Measure Your Results**

Success Starts Here!

"***You Deserve to be Rich*, ™"**

is for people who want to change their life's direction and find success in their own confidence, skills, background and passions. This book is for those people who also want to profit from it too!

It is no secret...you have talent and experience, background and expertise. You have energy and enthusiasm that until now has been devoted to making someone else rich. You have a vision of your success but you didn't know how to take advantage of, benefit from and profit from it...**until now.**

Some of the guidance you get is a direct link to your past experiences.

In this book, **"You Deserve to be Rich™"**, you'll find direction, tips and advice to form the business of "YOU!" You will find the methods and processes to help you grow as a business and find the profit in your expertise and authority.

It will help you use your life's experience, expertise, and passions to help other people do the same and...charge a respectable fee for your services.

After all, isn't that what consultants do, use their knowledge to sell something?

Those that choose to follow a path that they themselves question usually leads to an end that was predictable and distasteful. With that in mind, you should follow the leadership of those who have succeeded before you by using their experiences, failures and successes as a guide to moving on your own opportunities.

As an example, watch someone place their hand in a flame and get burned and you will likely not duplicate their actions in fear that you will suffer the same results.

We want to be like someone we respect and admire and are willing to change our life to accommodate that desire.

<u>Most people have a set of rules they follow based on their experiences, education, wants, needs and desires.</u>

"Only you have to power to choose your "Destiny on Demand"

- Mark Zupo

Chapter 2

Knowledge College

"Men make counterfeit money; in many more cases, money makes counterfeit men."

- Sydney J. Harris

"Will a college degree help or hurt your chances at starting a successful business?"

I can tell you from personal experience that some of our brightest minds in the world are being misidentified or incorrectly categorized because of the one-size-fits-all learning environment in the public school system. No one recognized my skills and virtues as a young person who couldn't wait to be an adult to exercise what I already knew as a child.

I recall sitting in a class in the ninth grade wondering why I wasn't allowed to speak when I had so much to say. As well, I was chastised by a teacher for helping another student with their work after completing mine in record time. The remaining time in high school was peppered with being told that I didn't have the intellect or aptitude to become a doctor or a lawyer and should choose to remain on the farm.

They suggested a trade school, construction, something where I'd be working with my hands. What a waste! The irony is that today I have employed hundreds of very well educated people and have trained as many more after their own failures as professionals. Go figure...

Given the opportunity, I'd turn education into a for-profit business, a capitalistic, revenue driven system. A competitive environment where each school is trying to attract customers, based on quality of customer experience and degree of skill and ability. Performance is the issue and success is the key.

I became a successful entrepreneur long before I ever had a degree. In fact, I didn't pursue a degree because I was a success without ever having one! I didn't have time because I was making money. After all, isn't that why you get a degree? To improve your life by earning the income that becomes necessary to support it?

As an entrepreneur, my success came without having a college degree or getting classroom training and didn't hurt my chances for starting a successful business. I don't think it is absolutely required but fundamentally necessary to be literate and knowledgeable. That means experience is as valuable as or more valuable than traditional education. Some people who do not have a formal education still have traits that lend to entrepreneurship and to the success it brings.

. . . I Have to Tell You about My Life up to Now

I grew up on a farm in Pennsylvania, about 13 miles from the nearest town with a grocery store, barber shop, and movie theater.

My first job was in a steel mill working to change the bricks in a blast furnace that made steel. I had to wear a fire-retardant suit because the bricks damaged by the last firing had to be removed before they cooled down. The temperature was nearly 400° degrees when I went in. The mill demanded I do this because time was money.

This job paid a whopping $1.90 an hour...worse than slave labor if you ask me. And I did it gladly because I didn't know any better. I saw a man crushed under a steel plate. I saw my friend, who was working right next to me, burned beyond recognition. I saw many accidents and incidents that changed men's lives forever; none of them for the better. I knew this was not the life for me. Now I know better because I have been mentored by other people on the secrets of earning more, a whole lot more.

I was taught how to succeed, what to succeed in, how I could find my own skills and expertise to speak on. <u>My advice was to find a mentor, find a mentor, and find a mentor!</u> When I did, the whole

<u>world opened up to me. I found my niche and now I am paid what I think I am worth, my real value.</u>

. . . The Benefits of the Perfect Business

There are many perks to this business. There are many social benefits, many monetary benefits and many rewarding benefits to this business. There are travel perks, social events, food, and of course, income. I have been on more than 100 cruises. More than half of them were completely free. Speaking has its benefits.

You Can Work This Business from Your Home

No special office or employees are required; no deadlines to report to work every day; no boss to argue with. Imagine you get a call to speak for a local group for a few minutes, maybe an hour and be paid very well for it.

You could accept from $1,500 for the average speaking event to a small local group to upwards of $10,000 for the same time for a much larger group.

Then, you sell them your products after the speech and the fun begins. <u>It was not impossible for me to make $5,000 a week for a few minutes work.</u>

Could you handle that? I'll bet you can.

<u>Most cruise lines use "enrichment speakers" for a few hours work and the cruise fees are traded for your time.</u> Imagine that, being boarded in the finest stateroom like a celebrity for a few hours of work.

. . . Did You know That...?

The majority of the income from public speaking doesn't come from the standing ovation at the end of your speech. Did you know most of the really "big" money comes from educational materials sold at the back of the room or online after an event? Your materials! Once established, the educational products will sell forever and earn while you sleep, while you vacation or while you are developing other materials for sale!

There are days you say to yourself, "If I had only known then what I know now". Absolutely, knowledge is paramount when you get it in time…and timing is everything.

Your Life is Big Business and... No One Taught You How To Run It!

The founding idea for this book was the realization that our lives amount to big business if we are taught how to manage, market and capitalize on them. Having worked to make other people rich was a lesson in managing them, marketing them and inspiring them to capitalize on their abilities, virtues and abilities.

Every successful person, male or female, has many of the same traits. These people are usually entrepreneurial by design. They are driven by their need to accomplish results of some sort, and they are only satisfied by achievements from their own efforts. These people are driven to achieve levels of success that are just as possible for any average person as they are for the high achievers. Everyone is divided into three groups. There are those who make things happen, those who watch things happen, and those who wonder what happened. Only one of these groups ever finds riches, happiness, success, or achievement.

In **"You Deserve to be Rich",** you will find a simple means of taking the focus off your employer, your relatives or your friends. We need to accept that we control our lives, which then has a profound effect on our successes. When you begin to look at yourself as a product, you can visualize putting your expertise and experience into a sellable format that others will buy to learn how to do the same for themselves.

> *"The bigger your mess...*
> *the bigger your message."*
> **John F. Kennedy -**
> **Cuban Missile Crisis**

Developing Your Credibility

- **Standing Out**

  -Passion, Power,
  Persistence, Purpose

People function differently. Remember the three groups:

- Those who **make** things happen.
- Those who **watch** things happen.
- Those who **wonder** what happened.

Which are you? This is the time for honesty. Giving yourself more credit than you deserve is only fooling you. If you don't like what you hear in your answer, now is the time to change it. It isn't necessary to be too hard on yourself; just be honest.

Your purpose - What's in Your Plan?

"Build your strengths by nailing down your weaknesses."
Mark Zupo – 2009

Desperation

If you are seeking fame, fortune, success and affluence out of a sense of desperation, any plan will ultimately fail. That's because desperate people make decisions in haste to try to achieve, as quickly as possible, the outcome they desire. This will never do.

Determination

When we are determined to make a quick decision, it usually is at the expense of critical thinking and decisive planning. Thoughtless determination never translates into an effective plan. This type of determination typically causes us to make a do-or-die decision or to perform an irreversible action due to a need to have accomplished something at any cost.

Dedication

Although dedication is an admirable trait, it is also a condition that lends to staying the course, when a better decision may be folding the cards and moving on to another option. We have options. We should use every resource at our disposal to weigh every decision and then to arrive at the correct decision, as opposed to the quick decision.

Inspiration

Inspiration, when making decisions and planning actions, is a valuable tool as long as the outcome and goal are well defined. Having a specific goal is the key that inspiration will lead to innovation and ingenuity. Ingenuity has been the lifeblood of American advancement in technology and in the modernization of our society.

Perspiration

Another key resource and essential quality in the planning process is your personal effort. You should make use of the physical attributes of your *perspiration factor* when making life-changing and self-empowering decisions. Success is appreciated to a greater degree when sweat-equity is a contributing factor.

Motivation

A final contribution to your planning process, motivation is a fundamental ingredient to achieving any goal and to determining the outcome of your decisions. Motivation may be the greatest factor in the planning processes because it is the catalyst for every action toward a predetermined goal. Unless you are motivated, success may be just a dream.

Visibility, Credibility, Profitability

Three critical elements to your success are visibility, credibility and profitability. *Visibility* creates the awareness of you and what you are presenting to an audience of believers, followers or students. Establishing visibility can be an expensive and tedious process, but it can be a vehicle for absolute success. Some considerations of the utmost importance are

a. You are true to your followers, students or believers.

b. You provide valuable content to them.

c. You nurture their participation by your contribution to their success.

d. You remain available to them to educate them and to foster their agendas.

Once your visibility is created through social media or personal appearance, the attributes that appeal to a following are the groundwork for establishing your credibility. Your *credibility* will allow you to present your ideas, proposals and initiatives. Your ideas will be accepted because of the trust established from your previous offerings and from the security in your word as reliable.

Methods to establish your credibility:

This is an important step in the process of allowing people to see you as a trusted resource:

1. Perspective:

Visualize your success as if it has already happened.

2. Philosophy

Develop a winning attitude that never waivers.

3. Personal Path

Take action steps that deliver results.

4. Position

Establish your authority with leadership.

5. Popularity

Manage your presence with other industry leaders.

6. Partnerships

Deliver your message with similar quality partners.

7. Progress

>Measure everything you do with your goal in mind.

8. Press

>Advertise who you are! Promote, Promote, Promote.

9. Performance

>Deliver more than is expected in quality, rather than in quantity.

10. Products

>Sell what you know. Who can do that better than you can?

11. Passion

>Have heart. It is the foundation of your success.

12. Pay

>You have to teach people to give you money!

You have to -

<u>teach people to give you money!</u>

Profitability will be the final condition to ensure success. This may sound a bit contradictory; however, unless you are and remain profitable, you cannot continue to promote yourself and to present offerings in the future. Promotion is expensive and presentation costs time, which also translates to expense.

Visibility and credibility, under the right guidance and in the right conditions, can and usually do convert into profitability. Keep in mind that the business world is a dynamic and ever-changing beast. It must be tamed at every turn lest it overwhelm both you and your profit machine.

"Love your work and work what you love"

Mark Zupo – 2007

Earning Income from the Work You Love

"A person's worth to society is measured by their wealth when in fact their wealth should be measured by their worth to society."
- Unknown

It is a mistake to allow any corporation to determine your value based upon what they think you are worth. Your value is what they determine your importance is to them; your worth is what they determine your significance is to them. Believe me when I say that the two are nowhere close in definition.

-Your Value or Your Worth

What is of greater importance is what *you* determine your value and worth to be? If value is **importance** and worth is **significance**, then consider the beneficiaries of those attributes and which is of greater importance to them. What you represent to your beneficiaries will be determined long after you are gone. Your value to them is your importance as it relates to their needs. Your value to your employer, for example, is that you sit at your desk and do your job. Your worth, however, is determined by who you are and what you represent. Your worth is your significance; it is your character, your enthusiasm and what you bring to the lives of those around you.

If you are a person who works for a business that you love, then you are the product of your own success. The "business of you" is vastly more important to your loved ones and associates than is a business you represent for someone else.

Can your children say that the gold watch you received after working for someone else represents who you are, who you have been for 30 years or more? A gold watch is a poor replacement for a legacy; it can never represent your value. However, your legacy as an entrepreneur, innovator, mentor, philanthropist, guide, educator, parent or guardian is and can be your legacy; it can and does represent your worth.

-Worth vs. Value,

-Want vs. Need,

-Deserve vs. Expect.

When you consider your **worth** to society, to a family and to a civilization in general, you are making a determination of the merit of your existence as it relates to their benefit. Your worth is your importance and usefulness in the name of some purpose. Your worth to the world is incalculable because you are continually delivering some benefit as you grow and develop.

The **value** you provide is of some significance to someone or something. Value represents the highest of quantity and quality.

Want comes from a deficiency or lack of something, such as money, freedom, independence and control. Wanting means you are absent a desirable trait or talent.

Usually one wants more money or a better education, but do we actually need more money or a better education to use what we already have? Interestingly, in countries where people live in poverty, what we think of as the necessities of life are virtually unknown; in these countries, want is also unknown.

Need is a requirement. Circumstances usually determine the degree of need, the sense of urgency. Do you want to be rich or do you need to be rich? Money may be a need, but it may also be a want depending on what your intentions are, such as philanthropy. Does the bearer of great riches <u>need</u> to give his money away or does the bearer <u>want</u> to give his money away?

Deserve is to be worthy of, qualified for, or have a claim to reward based upon an action or certain qualities possessed. You may deserve success, based upon some remarkable effort in a competition. However, you may not realize the success because another person was dominant in the competition. Perhaps his scores or actions were superior to yours. The lesson here is that we may *deserve* to win, but we may not get what we *expect*.

Expect is our ability to anticipate and hope for the outcome we want, which is often to be a success either in a single venture or in multiple projects. We can hope we will be rich, we anticipate we will be rich and we await riches! Interestingly, most positive, successful people talk about what they *expect* when they describe their future successes. They have some justification, founded in logic and reasoning, for their expectations. They are justified in their expectations because with positivity and experience comes with the confidence that success is likely.

Sometimes favorable results are simply the products of expectations. I recall a story about the legendary boxer, Mohammed Ali.

When he was asked by reporter Howard Cosell why he thought he was "the greatest boxer of all time," he replied, "Because I said so!" Ali's confidence was rooted in his expectation of beating all of his rival boxers. He expected to be victorious, which bolstered his own confidence and ultimately corrupted his opponent's confidence.

Leaving a Legacy

How to Re-Package your Life Experience

Your Uniqueness is Your Product!

"Just because you are sharing an experience with someone else doesn't mean that you are having the same experience."
- Mark Zupo – 2010

Here are 15 ways to sell what you know packaged as a product:

1. **Books**
2. **Video Course / Program on DVD**
3. **Audio Course / Program on CD**
4. **Digital eBooks**
5. **Tele-Seminars**
6. **Webinars**
7. **Live Seminars**
8. **Recorded Webinars**
9. **Affiliate Programs**
10. **Joint Ventures**
11. **Fundraisers**
12. **Corporate Sponsorship**
13. **Coaching Programs**
14. **Mentorship Programs**
15. **Public Speaking**

Video

Remember the 3-V's of Communication?

The 3-V's of communication demonstrate that the most important aspect of communication mediums is the visual. At 55%, visual communication is the most successful method to present to prospective buyers.

1. Verbal   7%

2. Vocal   38%

3. Visual   55%

"DISCOVER THE SECRET TO MAKE YOUR KNOWLEDGE SELL USING MY TIME-TESTED STRATEGIES!"

"Your life will never be the same once you know what to do, who to talk to, how to position yourself, how to attract more business, more money and more enjoyment out of life!"

You are just one step away from a dynamic and charged opportunity to JumpStart your success with *free* membership the

7-Level Success™ Series

Insider's Membership Club.

When you join the **7-Level Success™ Series Insider's Membership Club,** you'll get you own free copy of: ***You Deserve to be Rich*** which is jammed packed with tips to motivate and inspire you to greater success, bigger profits and a better life decisions! **Yours *FREE!***

Not only can you exploit the power of video marketing to propel your viewers into taking action, but you can quickly establish a defined brand of your own.

Videos add life to our marketing campaigns. They transform static, traditional campaigns into action-driven presentations that unleash our message in a powerful, dramatic way. Videos also give you the unique opportunity to communicate with your target audience in a way that puts you in touch with what is truly important to them, what motivates them and what will leave an everlasting impression.

However, videos have more value than just providing you with an interactive vehicle for your marketing message. Videos also help to increase the value of your products and of your brand. If you are involved in information marketing, you can instantly ramp up the perceived value of your products by adding in video-based components.

People often learn better when they are given a visual of both their tasks and examples of the end result. Creating dynamic video lessons or tutorials will instantly increase conversion rates and skyrocket your income.

So, now that you understand just how important high quality video presentations are to your marketing message, let's take a closer look at how you can develop laser-targeted video campaigns that speak your customer's language. After all, not all videos are created equally.

-Creating High Quality Videos

Imagine if you were able to personally welcome people to your website, to guide them through your information and to direct them to your order button. Imagine what that would do for your conversion rates! **Well, with videos - that's exactly what you can do.** Who am I? What do I contribute? Why do you need me? Videos can give you a call to action.

You can use videos in a number of different ways, including in sales pitches and tutorials, within your launch sequence to warm up customers and in the development of brand awareness. The more often people see you or hear you, the faster they'll recognize your brand.

The trouble is that many new entrepreneurs struggle with the technical aspects of creating high quality videos. They aren't sure what programs to use, how to edit videos, how to enhance the quality, or even how to create scripts or motions that guide viewers from one frame to another, retaining their attention every step of the way.

The great news is that even if you have absolutely no experience creating videos, there are tools and resources you can use to develop high quality, interactive videos in a matter of a few short hours. For starters, the majority of new computers come bundled with video production software already. However, if you really want to ramp up the quality of your videos, you'll want to consider purchasing an industry grade program, such as Camtasia™ or CamStudio™. These programs will help to add functionality to your videos, while making it easy for you to integrate sound (audio narratives, music, etc.), as well as to highlight important notes and to provide you with added flexibility in editing video content.

"Passion is the key...sharing is the path."

Mark Zupo - 2010

Own it...Live it...Believe it...Teach it

Characteristics of High Achievers:

- Have specific and measurable goals
- Take responsibility for their actions
- Want feedback to make improvements
- Share goals with those who can help them achieve
- Concentrate on high-payoff activities
- Prospect new markets and opportunities
- Set activities on a daily calendar
- Follow up on tasks, assignments and mission
- Review goals frequently to remain focused
- Emulate success in every detail

"The obstacles to success are not the things we think we need to be successful; It's getting rid of the baggage we already have that get in the way of our success."

Mark Zupo - 2010

Chapter 3

"Brain-Wished"

A man with money is no match against a man on a mission.

\- Doyle Brunson

When You Work for Someone Else

They determine what food you can afford to eat, what car you can afford to drive, what house you can afford to live in based on the money they think you are worth!

Let me say that again...**what they think you are worth.** Not what you think you are worth. It is up to you to determine your value! Not someone else.

Don't Be Surprised!

When people or groups hire you to speak they might shower you with gifts and prizes, vacations, invitations, event tickets and many more things as their way of thanking you for your well prepared and well delivered speech. They will admire you for your ability to move people to action, because you can motivate them, inform them, and inspire them.

... And, you might even be asked for your autograph!

I am still in amazement that people would want my autograph. The kid from the farm. It's true. And I gladly give it when asked. You can meet some every interesting people across this country and other countries as well. Did I mention that, too?

You also might be asked to speak in other countries around the world! Imagine your trip to Great Britain or Ireland, New Zealand or China is paid for when you are asked to speak for just an hour! Seems unimaginable but it could happen. Your social life will never be the same again.

> ...remember to ask me, when you see me next, to tell you about the story of how I sold my signature for $5 to buy food with the promise to buy it back for $5,000...and I did!

... How and Where to Start

"Build it and they will come." Sounds "korny" but there is a ring of truth to it for sure. However, it is simple enough when you know the tricks and tips.

First, you have to be visible and recognized for your abilities and that you are open for business. I have the tips for getting started that are essential for someone to ask you to speak and build their trust in you. It can be frustrating to determine if they fit the necessary criteria for you to speak.

Do they have the money and is it available when you want it? Do they have the need for your skills and topics? Have they read about you and determined you are the one for their cause? Have you qualified them before calling on them for more information?

Are you available when they need you?

In the beginning, there are many actions to take before the event ever takes place. It can be frustrating. Once you have established yourself as a professional, the people who seek you out expect to see and hear a professional.

What You Won't Do

You want to establish a celebrity status and "famous people" don't knock on doors!

You want people to knock on your door. You want people to recognize you as a professional, a celebrity, a professional-level speaker, an industry expert and an authority qualified to speak on the subject of your choice.

Your job is to be recognized everywhere and to put your name and professionalism where everyone can see it. You want people to hear about you, to call you and ask for more information about you, to inquire about your expertise and maybe hire you directly.

Let's talk about what professional speakers can earn. Let's talk about what the industry standard pay is and what you can command. Let's talk about the fact that this is not a get-rich-quick scheme…it requires some work, diligence and effort. Many people in every industry have earned great incomes speaking and by selling their educational and informational materials.

You can sell via TeleSeminars or Webinars as well as at live events. You can deliver "income driving" information via Webinars. You can give high-impact valuable information via Blogs and eZines and charge a fee for each product or service.

What you want to avoid is failure of any kind.

It has been determined that 8 out of 10 people who work for a living have considered starting their own business from home. As well, 9 out of 10 will never do it out of some misplaced fear of failure or seemingly insurmountable challenges.

REMEMBER WHAT I SAID ABOUT CHALLENGES;

CHALLENGES DELIVER OPPORTUNITY!

<u>This is huge!</u> The reason most only dream about it is because they don't know where to start. Because they are afraid of failure. Never be afraid of failure!

> **"Every challenge is an opportunity,**
>
> **The bigger the challenge...the greater the opportunity"**
>
> **Mark Zupo**

When I first wanted to become a pilot, I was told there would be years of training and examination, re-training and more training. The funniest thing about it was that I was afraid to fly!

That was OK, because I wanted it so badly, I could taste it. I knew that if I had a good mentor he or she would teach me not to be afraid. So I trained and trained, trained and practiced, practiced and practiced and eventually I became a commercial pilot.

As a result of my success I learned how to teach flying. That's when I really got good at it I learned the most important secret about flying. People aren't afraid to fly, they are afraid to crash! The same holds true about your life business. People aren't afraid to be an authority, *they're afraid to fail at being an authority.*

So, in order not to fail it is important that

you train, that you practice, that you get a mentor, that you seek guidance of a mentor with experience and that you see other people speak.

You can earn more in one hour more than most people that you know earn in three months of hard work for someone else. I don't want to completely focus on the money, even though it can be super but, that's what it's all about...right? Without money, life is a bit more complicated. With money life can be great fun and rewarding to all those around you. It goes without saying.

You must stand as an authority and professional to be demanded and sought after to earn the kind of sums that I mentioned before. This is big! I mentioned earlier that I have three degrees. Well, it is the truth but that isn't what made me successful. I didn't even start college until I was 44!

I always wanted to get my degree but didn't have the money, didn't have the time, didn't have the determination, didn't have the confidence and didn't, didn't, didn't and a bunch more excuses.

The reality was that I didn't want real success. That's why I named my mentoring program, "The 7 Level Success System". You must learn in order to earn. Why not learn from the best and brightest?

I can tell you flight training was unbelievably expensive and the return on my investment wasn't in money but reward and the confidence of accomplishment. As I live and breathe, I also learned it should have been about the money, too, to add value to the effort. I learned a lot about myself.

What Will It Really Cost?

It will take an investment of shorter time than it took to learn to fly. This can be accomplished in just a few weeks of the right training and guidance. When you have found the right information delivered by the right mentor, then you have a reliable method to help you succeed.

Don't forget, you are the one that has to do it though. No one can be on stage with you to hold your hand. No one will be holding cue cards or turn the pages for you.

There are no guarantees however...<u>Anyone can be successful at this with the right guidance and superior information boiled down from many years of experience.</u>

This alone will save you thousands of dollars that you will lose because you will never earn it! My initial assault at presenting myself as an authority was semi-successful and gave me the confidence to do it again, primarily because ...**I got paid for it.**

I couldn't believe it.

They actually paid me for talking to this small group of 45 people about "The Fear of Flying." My first public speaking event paid almost $1,500 dollars! I never earned $1,500 flying or teaching for an hour in my entire aviation career! In fact, it generally took three weeks of work to earn that much.

When I started flying I earned $100 a flight. It could be a 30 minute flight or a three hour flight. Both of which took all day and sometimes two days of my time and included what I paid for meals, etc. Sometimes I actually lost money!

Never Let It Happen

The thing you want to never let happen is to lose money by wasting it up front. You should know this before you start. Most or all of the information can be found in the advice from those who have been successful themselves.

> **Only the best qualified and experienced people can mentor to you and give you the information you need. The information I market is critical to your education.**

Some things you need to know are not only how to speak but how to market yourself. This is critical to your success. You've heard the phrase about real estate, "location, location, location"?

Well mine is "Training, Training, Training!"

No college ever taught me what I needed to know to succeed. What I learned was history. What I learned was how to think, how to evaluate and how to make decisions. What they didn't teach me was the formula, the path, the direction and the experience I needed up front. Yes, I am smarter because of it but it was a $150,000 lesson in failure. Just because you're good doesn't mean you will be successful. Good isn't good enough.

You don't need a degree to do this

You need guidance and direction. You need the right information. That is worth $1,000,000! It doesn't matter what the information costs. What matters is what it will **DO** for you.

"Show Me the Money"

The one thing I am certain about is that I always want the audience to listen to every word I say. This is because every word will motivate the audience to action.

The action I want is to not only deliver a message but have the audience feel comfortable with me and trust in me enough to keep coming back. You have to be credible, honest and trustworthy everywhere you appear whether on a website or in person.

This Is What I Learned At Great Expense

This is what you need to learn, too:

- How to write a book!
- How to create products!
- How to start a speaking career!
- How to earn while you learn!
- How to develop multiple streams of income!
- How to establish your credibility!
- How to turn your message to a hot selling topic!
- How to build a great website!
- How to drive interest to your website!
- How to make your own CD's and DVD's!
- How to use find your 3-foot radius
- How to develop your "elevator speech"
- How to outsource your work less expensive that you could do it yourself!
- How to joint venture with other successful people!
- How to find the clients that will pay you almost forever!
- How to develop your training program!
- How to sell your products on autopilot!
- How to demand and get the fee you set for your services!
- How to build a rock solid, self-perpetuating business on the Internet

- How to turn one speaking event into several more events!
- How to develop high content information that drives income!
- How to publish your book yourself!
- How to market yourself and your services online

Establish Your Brand Credibility

- How to package your materials the inexpensive way!
- How to create demand for your products before and after every speech!
- How to stand out as a entrepreneur, thought
- leader, and authority!
- How to find the hottest topics today!
- How to find your target market!
- How to determine your expertise!
- How to determine your credibility!
- How to maximize your exposure!
- How to make clients choose you over your competition!
- How to use electronic marketing to super-size your profile!
- How to create your brand, a brand that commands attention
- How to develop your website to attract wild global 24/7 attention
- How to convert visits to your website into sales

- How to "upsell", "presell" and "post sell" your clients
- How to find the industry contacts you need
- How to ask the million-dollar question that keeps the money flowing
- How to get on TV and Radio to maximize your exposure
- How to find a personal mentor who cares about you (I do)
- How to be a personal mentor to inspire others to their successes
- How to be in business for yourself, not by yourself
- How to eliminate the "Stinkin' Thinkin'" and motivate yourself

Give More Than Is Required

- How to create educational and informational material to generate income while you sleep
- How to start your own informational seminars
- How to be a mentor to another hopeful speaker
- How to pre-sell your products to clients before they ever meet you
- How to invoke the emotion of the audience to believe your message
- How to keep the audience glued to your every word

- How to use Viral Marketing to sell your speaking career campaign

- How to separate credibility from expertise
- How to remain personally attached to your message
- How to own your message and be recognized for it

Separate Yourself from the Rest

- How to change your potential to performance
- How to highlight the truths and delete the negatives
- How to JumpStart your speaking career starting "yesterday"
- How to deliver the 'hook" that sells every participant
- How to offer solutions as well as benefits
- How to change lives forever
- How to build confidence in your message
- How to learn 4-easy ways to earn while you learn
- How the number 3 becomes your best friend

Unleash the power of the Internet

- How to dominate your market
- How to be first in a new product, service or idea
- How to think yourself rich
- How to think yourself highly effective
- How to use power words that move people to action
- How to turn "challenges to triumphs"
- How to build trust in your products

- How to turn, "Would I, could I, should I" to "I will, I can and I do!"

By now you're wondering if I can deliver. I have combined and delivered information that is the hottest and most in-demand information on the market today. Not only will I deliver what I said I would, I'll give you much, much more too. Because I am genuine and I care about you.

> <u>Your success is paramount to my success. I believe in my success because I own it, I live it and I am sincere in my right to succeed. You must be as committed, too.</u>

You can't do this on your own. I want your testimony and your endorsement and your confidence and I will work very hard for that. This isn't rocket science; it is fairly basic information with a few secret twists. I'll give you the information and techniques that determine your income earning ability.

You have to use them at your best. There are no guarantees because I can't be there with you when you deliver a speech. I can't hold your hand or turn your cue cards. But I can give you the opportunity to learn the proper way of doing things.

Chapter 4

A Method to the Madness

Ben Franklin may have discovered electricity- but it is the man who invented the meter who made the money.
- Earl Warren

I deserve to be Rich

It wasn't arrogance or elitism. I thought I was just as good as anybody else and I could achieve anything that anyone else did if I worked hard enough. It took me many years of struggle to learn hard work wasn't the answer; smart work was.

Having struggled through trial and error in many business ventures throughout my life, I've been fortunate enough to learn a few key insights that would ultimately lead me to success and accomplishment. I was puzzled by the division of reasons why I wanted to succeed, notwithstanding the desire to be rich even before I understood what rich meant to me. It wasn't until I really understood the concept of choice that my reasoning to be 'rich" came to me.

That is why I decided to evaluate my understanding by the following reasons for wanting riches.

They are what I call, "To's". They are:

- The **need** to,
- The **want** to,
- The **have** to,
- The **choice** to,
- The **love** to
- And finally...The **call** to.

CHOICE

I believe the foundation for any desire is boiled down to the choice we make that is first and foremost our focus of intentions. Wanting to be rich is more complicated than just a desire to achieve wealth. Having wealth does not guarantee happiness and happiness does not guarantee wealth. More importantly, being rich is more a state of mind than a state of economics.

In my un-expert evaluation of my need to be rich, I believe the following categories of intention are crucial to success.

- **Need To   = Survival**

The need for wealth comes from a need to survive and the continued survival of your family. Without some money, you will certainly increase your opportunities to a shorter life. This comes from a lack of medical attention, shelter from the elements and food to sustain your health.

- **Have To   = Security**

    When you think you must have lots of money to be secure, it is an indication that you are insecure in your strengths and abilities to survive in a comfortable manner to which you have become accustomed to.

- **Want To   = Social Gain**

    The want to be rich is more of a self-seeking desire that gives you opportunity among your peers, superiors, friends, subordinates and in the social community.

- **Choice To = Self Growth and Development**

    One must make a conscious choice to pursue the avenue that might ultimately lead to success and riches. Choice usually translates to action and actions get results.

- **Love To   = Self Fulfillment**

    Having great regard for the things you've

acquired throughout your life reveals a humble appreciation for their value to you beyond simply worth based on price. A love to have riches indicates more of your appreciation for what wealth can do for others than what it can do for your self-fulfillment.

- **Called To = Inspiration**

I often have said, "I was called to be rich." I firmly believe that you deserve to be rich and having access to riches is a right rather than a privilege. A calling ignites your efforts and intentions to pursue the path that leads you to the goal you focus on. Your inspiration is your motivation.

Each of the attributes amounts to your responsibility and accountability as an achiever. Accountability can be good and accountability can be bad depending on how you govern your intentions, actions and choices. Whichever element of choice directs you to success or failure, each can be modified to make the outcome meet your desires.

I grew up on a farm in Pennsylvania working my chores and responsibilities because I was a responsible young man. Responsibility taught me many things. Responsibility taught me that accountability was the end result of my actions and if I didn't conduct myself responsibly, the accountability could be a severe lesson. Don't complete the chores you are assigned and you become accountable for your inactions. This has serious implications on a farm. As a young man under the rule of a demanding father...I felt that more often than not...the punishment didn't fit the crime.

"Failure is the major contributor to success"

Unknown

I could not have been more fortunate to have grown up with adult-like responsibilities. The lessons of farm life were many, were intense, and were lasting. One learns many things about life in every manner when growing up on a farm and usually takes it to their adult life in the form of character, respect, temperament, ethics, and personality.

No matter that I didn't stay on the farm and use these skills as my step-father would have liked, I carried each of them forward to find my passions and rewards in other arenas.

A true entrepreneur will find solution where seemingly none exist and triumph over it no matter the penalty, risks or challenge.

When we become educated to the value of everything we desire as opposed to the cost of the same, we can move beyond the blinders that keep us from success. In this book, you will find motivation, inspiration, guidance and situations that make you think.

Take what you learn from this book and run with it.

Preferably to the bank with what you will learn from experts and authorities who have built iconic lives out of a simple idea, a simple marketing plan, and some luck and guts. Everyone has enough life experience to make a fortune from it and most aren't aware of the power of their life experiences. It takes only a few minutes to discover that one's value is never as much as their worth until they learn how to market it to the masses.

Your computer – Your personal "ATM"

Self-Publishing your book

-Idea Producer One: What you're good at.

Make a list of 20 things you're good at. Don't think too hard about this. Maybe you're good at buying presents for people—you've got a knack for choosing just the right gift. Maybe you're a good cook or a good parent or a good swimmer or a good tennis player. Or maybe you used to be good at one or more of these things. For example: I grew up with horses and owned horses for many years. I'm good with horses, and I'm a good rider. If I saw a gap in the market for a horse book, I'd feel comfortable writing the book.

You get the idea. List at least 20 things that you're good at or have been good at in the past. For example, if you know you're an excellent gardener, even though you now live an apartment, list "gardening."

-Idea Producer Two: Your past experiences.

Experiences sell. If you've been abducted by little green men from Mars, it's a book. If you're a bigamist, it's a book. People have written books about their illnesses (see from challenge to opportunity below), their addictions and their pets. Browse through the bestseller lists to see what personal experiences people are writing about.

Don't get bogged down with this; list 20 experiences you've had that spring to mind. The easiest way to come up with experiences is to work backwards through the stages of your life or through decades. Again, don't take a long time over this. Set a time limit --- ten minutes is enough.

-Idea Producer Three: Your knowledge.

What do you know? Start by making a list of all the subjects you were good at in school. Then list all the jobs you've had – yes, part time work counts.

Also list:

- **Your hobbies.** Are you a keen Chihuahua breeder? Do you quilt? Take photographs?
- **Your current job.** What are you learning in your job that other people would pay to learn?
- **The places you've lived.** Your hometown may be boring to you, but guide books sell well.
- **Your family tree.** What special knowledge do your nearest and dearest have that you could write about?

Spend around ten minutes writing down as many subjects as you can that you have knowledge about.

-Idea Producer Four: What you enjoy most.

What do you love? People have written about garage sales, cosmetics, cars and vacations. If you love something, chances are that thousands, or maybe millions, of others will love it too.

Watch the newspapers and take note of current trends. Or better yet, listen to what your children are talking about or asking you to buy for them. Children tend to be up on what's happening.

With some education and assistance, you can publish a book in just a few days! With the advent of on-demand printing, you can go from concept to book-in-hand in about one week!

This doesn't mean, of course, that you can't write on perennial favorites like money, sex and exercise. These topics never go out of popularity, and a new twist on one of these is always a sure bet. The idea of writing about what you enjoy is that you will be bringing passion and enthusiasm to your topic. Enthusiasm is a must.

-Idea Producer Five: From challenge to opportunity.

You face challenges every day. Most are minor; some are major. If you've ever faced a large challenge, or if you're facing one right now, then consider that the things you learn could help other people. Whatever your challenge is, whether it's moving to a new house or confronting a life-threatening illness, other people face the same challenges, and in those challenges are the seeds of books.

Make a list of 20 challenges you've faced in your life. Anything catastrophic qualifies: the loss of your job, the threat of bankruptcy, the betrayal of a spouse. If you've had a quiet life, then make a list of challenges that the people you know have faced. Additional challenges you can consider include any habit you've broken, from congenital lateness to overeating. When you've finished brainstorming, you'll have dozens of book ideas. Winnow out the non-starters. Don't delete them; move them to another computer file. Call it "odds and ends" or "snippets."

"Every challenge delivers opportunity. The bigger the challenge...the bigger the opportunity."

- **Mark Zupo**

Checklist: Is this the right idea for you TODAY?

You've worked through the idea generators, and you have one or more ideas which you feel would work as a book. The next step is to scrutinize your primary idea carefully.

Consider your idea and look at this list of questions. See if you can answer "Yes" to all of them:

- ☑ Am I enthusiastic enough about this subject and my ideas about it to sell this proposal to an agent and an editor – and to readers?

- ☑ Will I retain my enthusiasm in the time it will take me to complete the book?

- ☑ Is there a market for my book? (I've checked Amazon.com and bookshops for competing titles. I'm convinced there is a market for my book.)

- ☑ I can find people with expert knowledge to interview as I write my book.

- ☑ Does my book provide solutions to problems?

If you can answer YES to most of these questions, you're set.

Chapter 5

Attitude -vs.- Aptitude

A nation that continues year after year to spend more money on military defense than on programs of social uplift is approaching spiritual doom.
Martin Luther King, Jr.

The Choices We Make

I believe the foundation for any desire is the choices we make, which is a result of our intentions. Wanting to be rich is more complicated than simply having a desire to achieve wealth. Having wealth does not guarantee happiness, and happiness does not guarantee wealth. Being rich is more a state of mind than a state of economics.

Based on personal experience, my evaluation of the need to be rich, I believe the following categories of intention are crucial to success.

- **Need To   =   Survival**

The need for wealth comes from a need to survive and to provide for the continued survival of your family. Without some money, you will certainly increase your opportunities for a shorter life. This comes from a lack of medical attention, of shelter from the elements and of food to sustain your health.

- **Have To   =   Security**

When you think you must have a lot of money to be secure, it is an indication that you are insecure in your strengths and abilities to survive in the comfortable manner to which you have become accustomed.

- **Want To   =   Social Gain**

The desire to be rich is a self-seeking desire that gives you recognition among your peers, superiors and subordinates, as well as in the social community.

- **Choice To =   Self Growth and Development**

One must make a conscious choice to pursue the avenue that might ultimately lead to success and riches. Choice usually translates to action, and action gets results.

- **Love To =   Self Fulfillment**

Having great regard for the things you've acquired throughout your life reveals a humble appreciation for their value beyond their simple worth based upon price. A love to have riches indicates more of your appreciation for what wealth can do for others than what it can do for your self-fulfillment.

- **Called To = Inspiration**

I often have said, "I was called to be rich." I firmly believe that you deserve to be rich and that having access to riches is a right rather than a privilege. A calling ignites your efforts to pursue the path that leads you to the goal you focus on. Your calling, your inspiration, is your motivation.

Each of these attributes of intention amounts to your accountability as an achiever. How you are ultimately held accountable can be good or bad, depending on how you govern your intentions, actions and choices. Whatever intention has initially directed you to success or failure can be modified to make the outcome meet your desires.

> *"Make your business your life and...*
> *Make your life your business"*
> *- Mark Zupo*

I grew up on a farm in Pennsylvania doing my chores and taking care of my responsibilities because I was a responsible young man. I **need**ed to complete my chores to get what I wanted to eat and to survive. I **had** to complete my chores to insure that the farm continued to grow and prosper. I **want**ed to complete my chores because I loved what I did and would ultimately get punished if I didn't!

I **chose** to complete my chores because it felt good to have some control. I **love**d to complete my chores because it was what my life was all about: helping others to grow. I was **call**ed to complete my chores because it was what gave my life meaning.

The responsibility I learned from growing up on a farm taught me many things. It taught me that accountability was the end result of my actions, and if I didn't conduct myself responsibly, the accountability could be severe. Don't complete the chores you are assigned and you become accountable for your inactions. This has serious implications on a farm. As a young man under the rule of a demanding step-father, I felt more often than not that the punishment didn't fit the crime. I did learn, though, that we must be accountable for all we do.

> ***"Failure is the major contributor to success."***
>
> **Unknown**

I could not have been more fortunate than to have grown up with adult-like responsibilities. The lessons of farm life were many, intense and lasting. A young person learns many things about life when growing up on a farm, and he takes it to his adult life in the forms of character, temperament, ethics and respect.

It does not matter that I did not stay on the farm, as my step—father would have liked, and use these skills. I carried each of them forward to find my passions and rewards in other arenas. There were many lessons from my youth that have stayed with me throughout the course of my life, but three were the most valuable to me.

Ignorance on Fire Beats Knowledge on Ice!

There are two important differences between motivation and inspiration. It will become important to learn what they are to lead you to success. I will teach you to understand why:

You are the Master of Your Success. You are the Master of Your Achievements.

You are the Master of Wealth, Freedom and Happiness.

I believe that there are only three types of people:

1. The type of person that watches things happen.
2. The type of person that makes things happen.
3. The type of person that asks, "What happened?"

<u>Which are you?</u>

    I teach you how to dispel the myths of failure, lack of control, and negative influences of other people. I will teach you how to find your "Real Dream System" to empower you with the strength and desire to "Be All You Can Be" and "All You Want To Be!" If it's been done before, then You can do it too! Be The First To Imagine It, And then...Achieve What You Can Believe!

    Here, you will learn three simple goal-setting methods that you can do before you are done brushing your teeth in the morning. You will learn how you can visualize your dreams and make them a reality. You will learn how you can do anything, be anything and achieve anything that anyone else can do, be and achieve.

"Oh, really?" you say. Yes really! If it has been done before, someone just like you did it. So what makes you think that you can't do it? They had money, they had time, they had help, they had….who cares what they had? You have the same resources within your reach and…all you have to do is ask.

When it comes to life and business, it is no coincidence that some people always seem to fail while others always seem to flourish. For sure, chance plays a role in everything. But as individuals, as business-owners, as thinkers and as parents, we have a significant degree of control over our lives.

Now, we can use the control that we have to influence outcomes negatively. Or we can use it to influence outcomes in our favor and in the favor of those we care about most. When we use our control poorly or when we don't use it at all, it should come as no surprise that our outcomes are bad. And when we use our control thoughtfully and carefully, it should be less surprising when we succeed.

Let me give you an example. At work, your employer considers you for a promotion; however, at the same time, she considers several of your co-workers for the same promotion. Now, as many do, you might immediately say, "There's nothing I can do to influence my boss in my favor. Instead, this decision will be determined by things that are out of my control." And, of course, when the day comes, you will not get that promotion. Instead, someone who pushed hard to demonstrate his worthiness for the position will get the job. You will be left wondering why that person is always successful and always gets promotions, raises, and the adoration of management.

You might even feel resentment toward that person, even though you consider him a friend. When it comes down to it, though, it wasn't your friend who caused you to miss the promotion (or at least not to give yourself the best shot at getting it). Rather, it was your own behavior that prevented your boss from seriously considering you as a candidate.

Fortunately for you, this book is all

about situations just like the one we described above. It's about feeling powerless when you're not, experiencing bad outcomes when there's no reason to and, finally, about making sure this problem stops.

> *"A diamond in an ugly setting... is still a diamond."*
>
> **Mark Zupo - 2008**

Most importantly, this book is about success. It is about extracting the characteristics of others that make them successful at work, in parenthood or in the workplace, and then adopting those characteristics for your own use.

So, without further ado, let's take the plunge. Today, you will stop telling yourself that you have no control over your life; and today, you will learn exactly what it means to take that control, grasp it firmly and use it to achieve success in all areas of your life. Set a goal, make a plan and DO IT!

> *"The greatest manifestation of productive effort is celebrated...at the Bank!"*
>
> - **Unknown**

Mentorship Programs: Follow the Leader

Learn from a model of success

You need to mentor others to change, create, empower, lead, build, enable, direct and guide others' lives to their specific independence and triumphs.

Mentoring versus Coaching

Definition: Mentor – *noun*

1. A wise and trusted counselor or teacher.

    An influential senior sponsor or supporter.

2. Definition: Coach – *verb/noun*

    To give instruction or advice in the capacity of a coach. A person who gives instruction.

What is a Mentor?

When we think of other people who helped us in our lives because of their experience and expertise or because of their interest or consideration towards us, we think of them as nice people who gave of themselves. We think of them as being kind to us or as helping us reach our goals or expectations. Whenever we were faced with a challenge or problem that seemed too hard for us to fix, those people used their life experiences as guidance to help us. This could have been as a child, in school, at home or even at work. Usually they were keen to point out talents that we didn't know we had or that we had not yet used.

Mentors come in many forms. They are teachers, parents, coworkers, bosses, other students, friends and relatives. In the past, people were mentored personally and in someone else's presence; but today's technology allows for mentoring to take place via many electronic means, and it eliminates the challenges presented by time and distance. The ability to mentor many people at one time via an electronic method is an invaluable tool and actually provides for many more opportunities for the participants. It helps to bring together people from many walks of life and cultural backgrounds.

As a mentor delivers the following:

- **Information**

    ✓ A Mentor will share his life and business experience and knowledge.

- **Methodology**

  ✓ A Mentor will deliver a precise and formatted methodology as a template for success.

- **Instruction**

  ✓ A Mentor will direct the mentees with pre-programmed direction and focus.

- **Opportunity**

  ✓ A Mentor will guide the mentee in various forms of opportunity with industry knowledge and experience.

- **Challenges**

  ✓ A Mentor will challenge and stimulate curiosity while building confidence and trust.

- **Support**

  ✓ A Mentor will build trust and achievement through his support.

- **Guidance**

✓ A Mentor will use his or her experience to guide the mentee in a focused and direct course to achieve the best outcome.

- **Goals and Expectations**

✓ A Mentor will give guidance and help to open lines of communication while defining a mentee's goals and objectives.

- **Advice**

✓ A Mentor will guide and help a mentee in reaching goals.

- **Models of Success**

✓ A Mentor will change, create, share, empower, lead, build, enable, direct and guide the lives of his mentees to their specific independence and triumphs.

Mentor Program Guidelines

A mentorship program offers a mentee the unique opportunity to develop a relationship with a mentor who is more experienced and skilled in the area that he wants to learn about. A mentor's experiences, perspectives and general wisdom can be effective tools for his mentee's success. Although a mentor and his mentee may talk frequently, the process begins with a delivery of valuable information or insight into the program.

For the program to work well and be a rewarding experience, there are some guidelines that must be met:

- Mentees should be able to rely on their mentors to keep them informed and up-to-date with all important information.
- A mentor should help a mentee develop a plan of action and set goals for success.
- Student-mentees should share their needs and wants and talk to their mentors about what they hope to gain from the program.
- A mentor program is a dynamic system to teach processes, and it requires mutual cooperation between both parties.
- Mentees should be willing to share effective feedback to their mentors, helping them to provide good content.
- A mentor is responsible for developing the mentee's fullest potential and strengths

and for eliminating weaknesses that inhibit growth and success.

> ***"Think like a winner and act like a champion,***
> *In other words, fake it till you make it!"*
> **Mark Zupo -2009**

It should be considered that although you might coach other people in the improvement of their lives, it is even more important that you build trust between you and your mentees.

I charge more than $1,000 per hour with a 3-hour minimum for authoritative mentoring. Mentoring people is one of the most lucrative revenue streams that you will ever find. The process to develop a mentor program is one that can be done anywhere in the world, at any time of the day or week.

-Systemization

The model for mentoring is to mentor many people at one time; although you are selling your knowledge at a cheaper rate because you have delivered the same information to more people at one time as opposed to a few people at one time.

As a mentor, you guide your mentees in the safest and most productive methods or paths that they should take. A clear example of a "mentor" program in the professional world is a franchise. There are many like McDonald's, drug stores, car washes and movie theaters. You can surely understand that a franchise is designed for the franchisees to be as productive and profitable as humanly possible. If the individual store owners succeed and make money, then the company that holds the franchise makes money and everyone is happy.

-Standardization

A huge benefit of a mentorship program is to set up your program so mentees are challenged to perform and to measure their performance. Without measurement and goals, mentees will falter und usually fail, even with your guidance. One of the challenges for someone who owns a franchisee is that he or she cannot alter or wander from the absolute prescribed method, product or practice of the franchise.

-Automation

Contact with your mentees is an

absolute must. Usually you will give them a private method to contact you with questions or problems. Email is one of the best methods to remain in contact to fully understand what the issue is so that the correct response is sent.

-Delegation

A comprehensive program is the best model for your success, as well as for the mentees' success. Pure and concise content, with an all-inclusive program, is the key to making a successful mentor program.

Delegation exists when the mentees have a support partner whose interest in their success is founded on mutual benefit. Once mentees are dedicated to their own success and commit to following your instructions, they will require a complete and comprehensive program to follow.

When you mentor more than one mentee, there is a synergy between mentees and mentor that will have a dynamic life of its own that will benefit everyone who participates.

"If you think you can or you think you can't... Either way you're right!"

- **Henry Ford**

Copy Success

-Get a Mentor, Get a Mentor, and...
<u>Get a Mentor!</u>

One method that I use to coach people who are reluctant to follow through with an assignment is to require them to sign a check made out for $100 to someone they don't like. Then the check is given to a loyal friend who wants to see them succeed and is sworn to send the check if they fail to perform. The key word here is DON'T like. The thought of giving away your money to someone you don't like is usually a motivator to achievement.

If ever you fail to complete a task assigned, the payment that is pending should scare you back into doing what you should do.

"To find success, you have to begin looking in the right direction, To get to the place where your success lives; you have to start where you stand."

- **Mark Zupo**

Chapter 6

"Wantre-preneur"

> There is only one boss. The customer. And he can fire everybody in the company from the chairman on down, simply by spending his money somewhere else.
> Sam Walton

"Can anyone learn to be an entrepreneur or are entrepreneurs just born?"

No. I don't believe everyone can be an entrepreneur.

There are three types of people in the world,

1. Those that make things happen
2. Those that watch things happen
3. Those who ask, "What happened?"

Just like animals, people can become domesticated through social programming and a flawed belief system making it difficult or impossible to ever be entrepreneurs. That is pretty blatant coming from a guy who teaches people how to become entrepreneurs. I'm actually selling a book and a program about how to become an entrepreneur, telling you that not everyone should read it or can do it. Remember, the first lesson is honesty, especially with yourself.

To be a successful entrepreneur, you have to have some natural instincts that most people are born with but seldom use. I don't think your instincts are genetic but you can 'inherit' them from your life experiences. Another key to success is to reprogram your beliefs to an absolutely defined strategy for success. However, there will always be people who will remain loyal workers in the system rather than elect to be entrepreneurs.

Building Your Life Product
Turn You into "The Product <u>YOU</u>"

-The Method

The method for turning your life into a product contains a few simple steps that involve a bit of technology and a bit of salesmanship. First you must learn what makes people wealthy and what keeps people wealthy.

- **What can I do to make a living?**
- **What do I know that will make me a living?**

First- *You Have To <u>Teach People to Give You Money!</u>*

The wealthy people of this world are different. In fact, they are dramatically different from the masses, which is what separates them from you. The one thing they know is that they have to teach people to give them money! Sounds crazy, right? No, not at all.

Wealthy people know the **seven** rules of attaining and retaining wealth:

1. Be decisive.
2. Be prudent.
3. Be responsible.
4. Be receptive to work that drives income.
5. Be generous by helping others attain wealth.
6. Be wary of luck without purpose.
7. Be voluntary. Ask and accept money as your reward.

What the rich learned was never taught in any school. The educational systems in America produce expectations. This is a sort of unconscious dependency on the system to provide for and to care for you instead of allowing you to produce for yourself. That is the exact opposite of entrepreneurship.

School is the first place that teaches you a form of measurement that inhibits your progress and growth as an independent person. The system is designed to let you know how they think you are doing, instead of allowing you to determine how you are doing. An opposing theory formulates the entrepreneurial mindset, and that is for you to determine what you consider real solutions to real problems.

This fosters imaginative thinking and ingenuity, the skills that are necessary for survival in the real world, as well as for survival in the business world. Being judged for work you don't like causes you to be obsessed with results and grading. It removes the joyful aspect of the process.

7 Money NO's

1. I'm bad with money.
2. Money doesn't grow on trees.
3. Only the rich get richer.
4. Money corrupts people.
5. Rich people are evil.
6. Money is hard to come by.
7. Money is the root of all evil!

8.

- **Running the Business of "You"**

➢ **Incorporate You**

➢ **Monetize You**
➢ **Create Your Business Plan**
➢ **Create Your Systems**
➢ **Name Your Board of Directors**

To begin with, you must have a plan to run the "You" business to achieve the goals you set for yourself.

"A goal without a plan is just a wish."
Mark Zupo – 2010

SuccessProcess 1-2-3™ - VISIBILITY

The First Step in the process is to have a means for people to find you. In this ever-changing world of technology, it is more important for people to find you in the easiest, fastest and most efficient way possible...via the Internet.

You must have a webpage that is the domain of "your name".

Specifically, you need something like mine, http://www.MarkZupo.com. Check out my main website and see what I mean. It is all about me and what I do. Rather, how I can serve.

You can and should have your own website with your name and your value proposition.

SuccessProcess 1-2-3™ - DESIGN

The Second Step in the process is to have a PRODUCT or products to sell: products that are specifically yours and no one else's, products that define who you are, what you're about or what you represent.

If You Have a Speech...

"If you have a speech...write it down; you have a book. If you have a book...market it; you have credibility.

If you have credibility...develop it; you have authority. If you have authority...protect it; you have income for life."

Mark Zupo - 2010

If you have ever been to a presentation at a convention center, a hotel meeting room or at a social function, you have heard someone speak about a topic that often seeks to separate you from your money. The topic isn't the important issue here. The presentation is.

When you listened to some person speak, you might have said to yourself, "I could have done that!" The speaker was poor, the speech was poor and the message was worse yet. The presentation skills of the speaker left a lot to be desired and you certainly could have done just as well or even better, right?

The point is, given the same opportunity; you can do the same presentation and, with some guidance and a little professional help, do it even better. The real point is that you can be paid handsomely for it. The only thing separating you from those of authority and credibility is visibility.

Someone who has written a book is automatically perceived to be an authority just because he wrote a book, any book about any topic! The easiest way to write a book is to write on a topic that is dear to you, a passion or something that you know a great deal about. Presto...you have just become a member of an elite group of authors. You are now recognized as a credible source of information and an authoritative source because...you said so!

When Mohammed Ali was asked, "Why do you think you are the world's greatest boxer?" He replied, "Because...I said so!" Your first assignment is to write a book. There is a book in everyone. There are huge benefits to writing a book. Just about every famous person you have ever heard of either became famous because he wrote a book or became more famous because he wrote a book. Just pick a name of someone you know that is famous and see what the title of his book is. I am sure he has one.

It doesn't matter what industry, what walk of life or what subject, be it political, religious, social or business; a book has been written by someone who has made money on it.

A book makes you an expert. It makes you an authority. A book establishes you as a credible source. There is no other medium that can deliver the results a book can. Your book makes you stand out in a world of experts because you are an authority in your industry or in your area of expertise. Some examples are:

- Robert Kiyosaki wrote *Rich Dad Poor Dad* and was virtually unknown until he wrote a book.

- Brendon Burchard wrote *Life's Golden Ticket* and was virtually unknown until he wrote a book.

- Tom Clancy wrote *The Hunt for Red October* and was virtually unknown until he wrote a book.

Timothy Ferriss wrote *The Four Hour Work Week* and was virtually unknown until he wrote a book.

A book, with a mere mention of it on the right media platform such as CNN, Oprah and the like, can propel you to national recognition. Once you get noticed, your name and business will take on a life of its own. Your book is used as ---

- ✓ **A Tool be recognized**
- ✓ **A Door Opener**
- ✓ **A Business Card**
- ✓ **A Method to Charge More Based on Perception**
- ✓ **A Device to Generate Revenue**
- ✓ **A Means to Develop Multiple Streams of Income**

Here is an example of how I help other people write their books *FAST!* This is an advertisement for my program that helps you develop a book.

Check out my program to help you write your book with lightning speed. It is called:

YourFastBook.

Mark Zupo

In the "YourFastBook™" workshop, you'll learn:

- How to write your book without ever putting pen to paper!

- How to market your book without ever paying a publisher!

- How to make your book available to millions with a click of a button!

- How to avoid the 10 most common mistakes authors make!

- How to protect yourself with this simple free technique!

- How never to pay a royalty and keep all the profit for yourself!

Don't Spend Years Trying to Write Your Book!

There is a Fast and Painless Way to Write a Book without having to actually write it Word for Word!

The Secrets to Writing & Selling Your First Book Fast! The Original How to "Write and Sell Your First Book" Workshop

Saturdays, 11-5

Have you ever thought of writing a book, but you just can't find the time? Now you can…because I will show you how to do it faster than you ever thought possible!

The **"YourFastBook™"** Workshop will give you all the tools you'll ever need to "blast" out a book in no time flat!

Still Not Convinced?

I am the author or co-author of more than 23 books to date. I am a "top-selling" author and credible authority on the self-publishing secrets that conventional industry publishers don't want you to know. Check this out! When you enroll in my award-winning workshop you'll get all this and more:

- How to write your book in one day!
- How to give your book an award-winning title!
- The three secrets to every author's success with future orders!
- How to turn your book into a "Money-Machine"
- How to make people pay five times what you paid for printing!
- Why the best books never get published and are lost forever!
- How to develop multiple streams of income from your book.

SuccessProcess 1-2-3™ - MARKET

The Third Step in the process is to develop your database, which is a list of people that follow you on social media websites like Twitter, Facebook, LinkedIn, and YouTube.com™ and so on. You can develop a database by offering a free informational product in exchange for an email address.

This may be the most important step in the process of selling you as a product. This strategy works very well and great attention should be paid to these steps to get the maximum outcome from it. Why will this work so well for you? Aligning yourself with an already respected marketer or easily recognized authority gives the impression of credibility based upon that association.

These authorities and celebrities in the business world may also have established lists of their own that can be "rented" to you in exchange for some consideration. You can see evidence of this with Taco Bell and Kentucky Fried Chicken restaurants in the same building.

There can be a shared promotional opportunity between you and another recognized person or company. The association gives an implied endorsement of you and your products.

Once you have focused on a market to direct your campaign and you have developed a product to sell, you then begin to collect partners who are willing to promote you and your products. Then you establish a list of their clients to market to for shared exposure or profit. When you enlist new partners to help drive traffic to you, you establish and maintain the new list of patrons from that point on.

Any new interested opt-ins, those who opt to receive information about you and your products, are seeking to satisfy their own curiosity. Some will stay and some will go. If you deliver great content, products or services, you will get great things in return.

Here are seven simple steps to successfully building and monetizing a list:

1. Specifically define your target market.

Define, with precision and specificity, who you are selling to.

2. Create an irresistible lead-generating magnet.

Get their attention and deliver unbelievable value.

3. Create an email marketing campaign.

Capture and store permission-based opt-ins.

4. Convert your new leads from an opt-in squeeze page.

Publish a squeeze page that hits hard and demands action.

5. Drive traffic to your opt-in page with social media.

Use social media in every form to direct attention to your site.

6. Instill sincerity and trust in your new list of interested opt-ins.

Build trust, establish credibility and maintain authority and respect.

7. Monetize your list with front and back-end sales.

Solve their problems. Create, promote and sell what they want. Offer more; offer it again.

The point of establishing your own list is to market to those on it forever. Let's do some simple math to establish just how important everyone is to you. Every subscriber you have collected who pays you $10 dollars will add up to a thousand dollars very quickly.

For example:

1- A subscriber pays you **$29 dollars** a month.

2- More subscribers pay you **$29 dollars** and do so for month after month.

3- New subscribers pay you **$29 dollars** and add to your database of people who will buy more from you down the road.

Let's look at this example:

Add this up: You get 50 subscribers to your newsletter or program. Once you have 50 subscribers, multiply each of them by $29. That equals **$1,450 dollars**...a <u>month!</u> When you have 50 customers who have bought from you once, you can market other products to them over and over again.

A second example: You already have $1,450 dollars a month from them. Now, sell one or more products to them as well. Let's say you sell three additional products at $24 each.

3 additional products - 25 X $24 dollars = **$600 dollars**...a <u>month!</u>

Now you have a possible additional **$600 a month**.

Consider this: $600 dollars plus $1,450 dollars = **$2,250 dollars**...a <u>month!</u> All this comes from selling to people once. This can be repeated many times over.

One key strategy they use is to up-sell you, to suggest upgrades and more expensive products, almost immediately after you have made a purchase.

As you can see, the earnings will add up very fast to a point when you couldn't stop it if you tried. Imagine if your first product was priced at $39 dollars or $47 dollars instead of $24? Do the math and you will discover just how important every subscriber can be.

These are people you may never meet individually and pay you a small amount but collectively they pay you a great deal of money.

Do The Math!

Chapter 7

Bear Poop and Panache

Marketing Yourself

**Spread the word about you with
The Four Step Process to Selling You:**

1. You the Positioner

Positioning is the requirement that you establish yourself as an authority or an expert. What is the process for that? You establish your authority or expertise based upon your experience and education in an area in which other people aren't as skilled. You can read as few as twenty books on any subject. You can say confidently that you know more about that subject than most of the people in the country. Once you're established in a field, if it is in print, it is generally believed simply because it is in print. This is how you establish your authority.

2. You the Packager

Packaging yourself is a simple matter of recording your presentations in one form or another and placing them on digital formats, book text formats and audio formats, such as a CD, a DVD, a book or an Mp3 recording.

3. You the Promoter

Promoting yourself can be a challenge; however, it has and can be done effectively. There are many means, through radio advertising and radio interviews, television interviews and print mentions. There are my favorites as well, such as webinars, Tele-seminars, word of mouth and more.

4. You the Partner

Partnering is simply a joint venture between you and another like-minded person or company. You could choose to "piggyback" your advertising or information to be promoted on another person's list. This is a very effective method for someone without a starting list of his own.

5. You the Author

The next step is to write a book. Writing a book gives you an unbelievable amount of credibility simply because of what most people see as the complexity of writing a book. That, in itself, is a huge accomplishment for most people. Soon, you'll learn that it is an easy process you can accomplish in a short amount of time. You'll also see that it is probably the one single thing that you can do to enhance your credibility, authority and recognition. Once you have committed to writing a book, your focus is to market it. Marketing is the absolute key to your success as an author. Just ask any publisher what the biggest costs are associated with your book and he will tell you marketing. It costs pennies to actually print your book and thousands to market it.

If the traditional publisher doesn't think your book will generate a substantial income, you will never get published! I am sure you have heard the nightmare tales of an author submitting hundreds of manuscripts in hopes of being published, only to be turned down as many times! Today, through technology and automation, the game has changed. It is now possible to draft, write, transcribe, print and sell a book in less-than 30 days!

-Social Networking the Globe

3-V's of Communication

1. Verbal   7%

2. Vocal   38%

3. Visual   55%

*"Early to bed and early to rise...
work like hell and advertise!"*
- Ted Turner

Think Marketing, Marketing, Marketing......

There are only <u>three</u> ways of building wealth today:

- You can either take a one-time job and **get paid once a week for every week you work** (after you work).
- You can work-for-hire (contract), which is usually limited to a one-time deal.
- You can build your own business and earn **residual income**...virtually forever!

The last method is obviously the most desired method of building wealth, earning residual income whereby you can earn <u>over and over</u>, even though you only put in the effort once!   Let me repeat that...***ONCE!***

Actors, writers, musicians, singers and inventors are marketers who earn residual income from their past accomplishments. Those accomplishments pay them virtually forever, and yours should too! There are a few recurring income secrets you can learn that, as soon as you put them into practice, will change your life forever. The great thing about them is that they are much easier than what you are doing now. The secret I will reveal to you is...<u>it is no secret</u>. That's right. It is a simple process of marketing that the rich study and that the wealthy have put into practice. This is the same method that you can use too.

It starts with

- ✓ Duplicating Yourself
- ✓ Marketing yourself
- ✓ Marketing What You Know

Duplicating Yourself

7-Secrets to Profit from Your Executive Life Experience!

System-ate. Automate, Delegate, Replicate

1. **Do you have a Message?**

   Everyone has a story to tell and some have a few more than that. If you can put your message into an outline format and present it to more than one person, you have a speech!

2. **Who are you?**

   Are you a person others look up to? Are you

a person who leads other people? If you are, you have the ability to teach others and delegate tasks that help spread the word about your message.

3. What are you?

Are you a person with the ability to speak, to present, to organize thoughts and processes? If so, you can take your knowledge and experience and put it into an automatic system to help other people...for a price.

4. What is your purpose?

Are you driven to deliver your message because it makes you feel better and it helps other people? Are you motivated by fame or success or by the confidence that you will make a difference? If so, coaching others is absolutely for you.

5. What are your passions?

Is there something that you have always been passionate about? Is it something that drives you, the very thing that you live for? If so, you have knowledge and experience that someone else with the same passions may lack in their endeavors.

6. What can you do for others?

What is the one thing that you know that you can share with others that would improve their lives? What is it you have discovered that has been withheld from people, the information that would make a difference in their lives if they just had the knowledge?

Knowing that your simple offer of information has the power to change a life will reward you with confidence in yourself. That reward, however, is small compared to the reward of satisfaction you'll receive knowing you've made a significant impact on someone else's life. "Can you help me? Can you help me help myself?" If so, coaching is for you.

7. What do you have to offer that is of value?

Is it possible that you know something that would be of great value to someone else - even if you think it is so simple that you never give it a second thought?

The concept of value is in how useful the information is that you give. How the value of that information is credited in another person's mind is based on what it does for him.

The information that contains the highest value is determined by the person who gets it, not the person that gives it. That said; never underestimate the value of your knowledge or experience, no matter how small it seems to you.

Social Media: **What is my "Webinality?" Do I have a social image?**

You can make money helping other people!

- Can you package your message?
- Can you change someone's life?
- Can you inspire someone's life?
- Can you motivate someone else to greatness?

Your secret to success have a vision of who you are and who you want to be

Life Mapping: A Vision of Success

Success is more than economic gains, titles, and degrees. Planning for success is about mapping out all the aspects of your life. Similar to a map, you need to define the following details: origin, destination, vehicle, backpack, landmarks, and route.

Origin: Who you are

A map has a starting point. Your origin is who you are right now. Most people when asked to introduce themselves would say, "Hi, I'm Jean and I am a 17-year old, senior high school student." It does not tell you about who Jean is; it only tells you her present preoccupation. To gain insights about yourself, you need to look closely at your beliefs, values, and principles aside from your economic, professional, cultural, and civil status. Moreover, you can also reflect on your experiences to give you insights on your good and not-so-good traits, skills, knowledge, strengths, and weaknesses. Upon introspection, Jean realized that she was highly motivated, generous, service-oriented, but impatient. Her inclination was in the biological-medical field. Furthermore, she believed that life must serve a purpose, and that wars were destructive to human dignity.

Destination: A vision of who you want to be

"Who do want to be?" this is your vision. Now it is important that you know yourself so that you would have a clearer idea of who you want to be; and the things you want to change whether they are attitudes, habits, or points of view. If you hardly know yourself, then your vision and targets for the future would also be unclear. Your destination should cover all the aspects of your being: the physical, emotional, intellectual, and spiritual. Continuing Jean's story, after she defined her beliefs, values, and principles in life, she decided that she wanted to have a life dedicated in serving her fellowmen.

Vehicle: Your Mission

A vehicle is the means by which you can reach your destination. It can be analogized to your mission or vocation in life. To a great extent, your mission would depend on what you know about yourself. Bases on Jean's self-assessment, she decided that she was suited to become a doctor, and that she wanted to become one. Her chosen vocation was a medical doctor. Describing her vision-mission fully: it was to live a life dedicated to serving her fellowmen as a doctor in conflict-areas.

Travel Bag: Your knowledge, skills, and attitude

Food, drinks, medicines, and other travelling necessities are contained in a bag. Applying this concept to your life map, you also bring with you certain knowledge, skills, and attitudes. These determine your competence and help you in attaining your vision. Given such, there is a need for you to assess what knowledge, skills, and attitudes you have at present and what you need to gain along the way. This two-fold assessment will give you insights on your landmarks or measures of success. Jean realized that she needed to gain professional knowledge and skills on medicine so that she could become a doctor. She knew that she was a bit impatient with people so she realized that this was something she wanted to change.

Landmarks and Route: S.M.A.R.T. objectives

Landmarks confirm if you are on the right track while the route determines the travel time. Thus, in planning out your life, you also need to have landmarks and a route. These landmarks are your measures of success. These measures must be specific, measurable, attainable, realistic, and time bound. Thus you cannot set two major landmarks such as earning a master's degree and a doctorate degree within a period of three years, since the minimum number of years to complete a master's degree is two years. Going back to Jean as an example, she identified the following landmarks in her life map: completing a bachelor's degree in biology by the age of 21; completing medicine by the age of 27; earning her specialization in infectious diseases by the age of 30; getting deployed in local public hospitals of their town by the age of 32; and serving as doctor in war-torn areas by the age of 35.

Anticipate Turns, Detours, and Potholes

The purpose of your life map is to minimize hasty and spur-of-the-moment decisions that can make you lose your way. But oftentimes our plans are modified along the way due to some inconveniences, delays, and other situations beyond our control. Like in any path, there are turns, detours, and potholes thus; we must anticipate them and adjust accordingly.

Chapter 8

Life, Liberty and the Pursuit

If you don't have integrity, you have nothing. You can't buy it. You can have all the money in the world, but if you are not a moral and ethical person, you really have nothing.
Henry Kravis

Branding your Life

You're brand is your reputation and it encompasses the following:

- **Your personal reputation.**
- **Your unique promise of value.**
- **The permission to be yourself.**

Why did personal branding begin? Personal branding grew from a faster business world which is increasingly driven with technology and innovation. As well, a new niche of personal egos has been created from the increasing desire to be recognized for our unique strengths and contributions.

Branding is all about the image of a business. In this case, remember, the business is you. This image should not only include style, emblems and logos, but it should also include the image of quality. The image perceived should be one of total quality and reliability.

From this point on, when we discuss a brand and a reputation, we will refer to you as the business and, respectively, the business as you.

When we think of certain political figures, movie stars or television personalities, we usually recognize them by their names: Oprah, Madonna, Sting, Sarah Palin, Rosie, Chevy Chase, Donald Trump, Connie Chung, George Clooney, Ice-T, Regis…etc. You recognize exactly what they represent when you hear their names.

Branding is about the individuals or the businesses and what makes them different from their competitors. The purpose of a brand is to distinguish you from your competition.

Once you have a distinguishing impact that establishes your personal brand, an advertising campaign can be much more effective.

Branding includes many factors which help you be successful:

A website *"webinality,"*

Marketing efforts

Anything that gives a company an identity

Consumers, because there is a psychology in what motivates their purchasing decisions, wholeheartedly trust a corporate image. A small company with a brand, when it practices the right techniques, looks just as good as any large corporation who has spent millions of dollars to be recognized in their industry. Brands enhance your confidence as a business owner, and they build confidence in the consumer's mind. Branding indicates that you really can deliver what you promise.

Branding offers the perception of consistency. Inwardly, it gives direction to employees to deliver on established consumer expectations. Outwardly, a brand's consistency provides visibility that represents the professional appearance which will remain in the memory of a consumer.

One concept that consumers often attach to a brand is called brand equity. A brand is often considered to be an asset. For example, if you have developed a brand that is well known for being a top distributor of computers, your brand will be worth more than the brand of your competitor who is known to provide lesser-quality products.

Branding Basics

Branding is about the person or the business, and what makes *them* different y*ou*. Distinguishing yourself from others is a critical step in creating the "**Business of You**." I have created seminars and my Mind Your Business ™ training resources to teach you how to find your strengths and demonstrate your uniqueness to others, which will make you, stand out from your competitors.

Branding is all about shaping customers' perception of you or your company. Your brand is the promise that you make to customers. The ultimate goal is to spark an emotional connection and to create a positive feeling, resulting in customer loyalty to a specific product.

Most customers remain true to products they enjoy. It is very common for a customer to be impressed with a brand and continue to buy a product based upon that brand. Ultimately, you want to create these feelings of loyalty to bring the customers back for more. The benefits of personal branding are

- Self-understanding of what makes you valuable
- Visibility and presence to help achieve your goals
- Differentiation from your competition
- Wealth that comes from strong brand recognition.
- Continuity from resolve to success.

Know Your Mission and Vision

The mission and vision statement of your company should uphold excellence in providing a quality product to your customers. These are statements about your company regarding the ultimate goals you wish to achieve. Many companies focus their vision or mission on their employees, while others extend their mission outward to the customers. There should be a fine mix of both.

The vision and mission statements are very important for every business, no matter how big or small. As you craft your vision and mission statements, ensure your brand works well and that it matches what you say you want to deliver. You must also determine the benefits and features of your business and have a clear picture of their impact. You will need this information when you focus on developing your brand.

Many customers do not read vision or mission statements. However, that doesn't mean that you shouldn't take these statements seriously. Your vision and mission statements both are a part of the branding process because they define what your company is all about. These two statements need to be believed and practiced by all the employees and the staff of the company.

Benefits and Features of Your Products or Services

A big part of creating a brand for your business is showing customers why your products and services are the best to buy.

Differentiation occurs by proving the benefits of doing business with you to the consumers. Determine the benefits of what you are offering. Why do customers benefit when they shop with or buy from you? You will have a very hard time establishing a brand if you cannot determine the differentiating benefits of your products or services.

The specific features of your products and services are also important. Determine the specific features; which ones stand out from the rest or provide the biggest benefit? These may be a target for your marketing campaign.

Know Your Customers' Perception

Branding is about customer perception...and perception is everything! When you want to create a brand, you want to create a perception that you are the best, that you provide quality and that you deliver what you promise.

When you are building a branding campaign, it is important to have a good idea of what the customers currently think of you. Today, customers may not know you exist, or they may have a negative attitude toward your business because you haven't been delivering top-notch products or services. You might think customers absolutely love you, when they are really avoiding you or your products because of the poor quality of your product. Knowing what the customers think is very important. Creating a brand based upon customer input can be successful, especially if you change the design of something for the customers. This gives them a sense of ownership, and it shows them you really do care.

Know your Audience

Audience is everything. If you do not know your audience, you cannot begin creating a brand for a product or a company. There are many reasons that your target audience must be considered. Knowing your audience well will work for you over time.

The audience is the targeted customer base that you are hoping to reach. Audience considerations may include gender, age, geographical regions, and more. The age of an audience must be considered when branding. If you are targeting a younger and hipper crowd, they may want to see a brand that is vibrant and trendy.

If your audience is older and more sophisticated, they may be looking for a brand displaying more professionalism.

The gender of an audience is often an issue, especially if you are selling gender-specific items. However, when you create a brand for men, remember that you can create ad campaigns targeting women to purchase the products as gifts for men.

A customer's income isn't something that many businesses who are developing a brand think about when they consider their audience. This is often where companies go wrong. If you are selling a video gaming system for several hundred dollars in a local store, and the average income of families in the area is less than $25,000 a year, families may not be able to afford the product. You cannot sell an expensive product to a poor audience.

Also, people with a very high income may not consider purchasing a cheap product. The value of your brand must match the income of the people you think will be your primary target customers.

There are many things about your audience that you must know when you are creating a brand. If you do not have a clear understanding of your audience, you will fail. It is important to narrow down your target audience based on age, gender (only if specific), geographical region (only if specific) and income level. Once defined, you will know your specific audience, for example, 20- to 30-year-old, left-handed, male golfers.

Some brands may not be this specific. However, the more you can narrow down your audience, the more your brand will separate you from the competition. You will have fewer competitors with whom to compete.

Logos

Today it is common for people to say that a logo is everything when it comes to branding. This couldn't be further from the truth. A logo is important in many ways when branding; however, it is not where the rubber meets the road. A logo is one of the smallest forms of branding.

It is common for companies not to have a graphical logo that represents their company.
They may just have the name of their business in bright, basic letters in front of the store. Many online site owners do the same and simply write the name of the website in bold letters at the top. Ever hear of IBM or AT&T?

A logo may be a creative way of writing your company name in bold or italic lettering, in a special font, or in different colors; it may even contain a picture. An iconic logo is the golden arches of McDonald's. This is a symbol that everyone recognizes. When approaching the arches on the side of the road, people immediately know the restaurant indicated.

Does a Logo Really Help You Sell?

There is a lot of hype about logo creation. The web is saturated with companies offering to design the perfect company logo. Logos do not help you sell products. They are not responsible for increasing revenues. No one buys a product because the logo is cool or professionally designed. They do, however, have value.

Logos create a positive impact for a business. A company with a logo versus a company that does not have a logo looks more professional and appears to be a more credible place to shop. This is because a professional logo creates an image. For example, employees wearing plain blue shirts in a store do not look as professional as employees wearing the same plain blue shirt with a company logo stamped on the top left chest area.

Logos are a part of the perception you create for your customers. Your goal in designing a logo is to create an image that has an emotional impact with the customers. This doesn't mean to add an emotional picture or throw in a tagline to make people cry.

Taglines, like logos, should have an impact; they should make a promise you are going to deliver. Pictures should not be in logos at all; however, if you choose to put one in a logo, ensure it is small and not too busy.

Building Trust and Recognition

Building and earning trust, which is also building recognition, can be a difficult task in the branding process. There are many ways that you build trust and recognition. However, you must start within the organization; within the organization you can begin to build the trust that will lead to recognition. You can then work your way out to the customers and the competitors.

When you are creating a brand, you need to be consistent in everything that you do. Remember, your brand is your image, and inconsistencies will poorly impact the consumers. The primary question that you should ask yourself is whether or not you deliver everything you promise to your customers. Your answer should always be yes. Delivery on your promises should be consistent at all times.

What is Your Personality?

Your personality has a lot to do with your brand. You should make sure that your personality matches your brand.

It is wise for companies to hire a brand manager so there are not problems with personalities conflicting with a brand. The image of the company needs to be based on what looks good for the company, what is attractive to the customers, and what will sell. Your individual personality should not mix into the brand.

Some people say that you are your brand and your personality should shine through your brand. However, there is a fine line with this theory. A branding manager is a good option because this person can be impartial when he helps you create an image; he will have an unbiased point of view and not allow individual personalities to interfere with the creation of a brand.

Competition

There are many things to consider about your competition when you are designing a branding campaign. Many businesses fail because they do not consider their competition.

You need to do proper research on your competitors, learn what makes you different and determine why customers should choose you. Understand that there really is no competition. You never want to look the same as the rest of the companies in your industry. Don't be afraid to step outside of the box and be different. This is how consumers will remember you. If you all look the same, they will think it doesn't matter where they go to make their purchase.

Establishing Brand

Once you have determined your mission and your vision, your audience and your difference from the competitors, you can begin to establish your brand. There are many things that you need to do to establish your brand so people will begin to remember your name. These things include getting inside of the customers' minds, obtaining endorsements, finding hot prospects and using public relations firms to your advantage. These few things will go a long way to establish you in the market.

Establishing a Place Inside of the Customer's Mind

One of your biggest goals in the branding process is establishing a place inside of the customers' minds.

Your goal is to prove to customers that they have a need for your product or for your service. Customers must find a reason why they need you. The branding techniques will tell customers that your product resolves a problem, fulfills a need and makes their life much better. When you get inside the customers' heads, customers will believe they absolutely have to have your product.

Just as you hear many infomercials talk about how someone will become rich if he uses a product or how his health will be better, you need to establish the benefit to the customers so you can make them truly believe that their lives will be much better when they use your product. This also means that you have to build trust and credibility with the customers.

Endorsements

Consumers listen to public figures. When you have the ability to get an endorsement on a product, you need to take advantage of it. However, you cannot wait for an endorsement to come to you. There are many ways to get endorsements. You may attend events where a public figure is going to be.

This includes getting back stage at concerts or shows where you can have access to the person. You also can call celebrities' managers and talk to them about getting an endorsement for your product. One thing to keep in mind about endorsements is that you need to find someone who matches your audience. If your target audience is teenagers, you want to find an endorsement that the teenagers know and trust.

Find someone who the teenagers think is hip; they will want your product when they learn their idol uses it. The last thing you want to do is get a product endorsement from an older individual, even one who is well known and respected by an older audience, whom the teenage audience has never heard of. This would be a waste of money and time.

Using Public Relations Pro's to Your Advantage

Media attention needs to be used to your advantage. There are many ways to do this. One thing to keep in mind is that your product and your brand do not have to be fully established to gain the attention of the media. You can use the media to help you get established.

Using press releases is one of the best things you can do to get the exposure you are looking for and to help you create a place in the industry. A press release is usually used for announcing grand openings for new businesses, new product launches, big sales and events, or anything else knew that is happening within a company.

The elements of a press release should include the event itself; why people will benefit going to it; and the location, date, and time of the event. If you don't tell people where to go, it will do you no good. You should also provide your company contact information in case the media wants to call you to get an interview or to write a story on the company. Customers may have questions. No contact information could cost you a lot of business.

Also, always include your website address in a press release so people can go to your site and learn more about who you are.

Press releases are sent out to as many media outlets as possible to target the audiences you are trying to reach. These media outlets include news stations, newspapers, magazines, radio stations, and more.

When a media outlet receives a press release, they may do a few things. They may immediately respond and use it for the next big story that hits the press. They may put it aside for a while and then use it when they need a story. Alternatively, they may do nothing at all.

Sending out a press release doesn't cost a business anything. It is cheap, and it is always good to send a few out, even if the media is not interested. The point is that you must, at least, try to use public relations to your benefit. It may be only one event or announcement you have about your business that is used by the press. That one small bit of exposure could go a long way for you.

Establishing Company Identity

Establishing your identity is very important when you are fighting for a place in a market or in a certain niche. You may know exactly who you are, but you need to get your name out there for others to be aware of your existence. There are many ways you can establish an identity in a local community or around the world.

Giving Free Information

Many companies upset customers because they want to charge money for everything. This leaves customers walking away with a bad taste in their mouths and only causes the company to look dishonest or greedy. There are things that you can give away for free, especially when it comes to information. You cannot, however, teach a customer everything you know in just a few minutes of talking to them or in a few pages that they can read. Many businesses practice giving free tips and advice through flyers and brochures.

You may want to place a few useful tips on the back of your brochure. This will help build credibility and trust with customers, demonstrating that you are not greedy and are willing to help them achieve certain goals. It will also prove to them that you actually have the knowledge to perform certain tasks within your company. You don't have to reveal secrets of the trade, but you can give out helpful information that is useful.

Giving useful information, for example, may include offering tips and advice when you are out on a service call in a home. If your company offers plumbing services and you are on a call for frozen pipes under a home, you may recommend the customer leave the water dripping overnight. This type of advice is useful to customers and will help them avoid a burst pipe.

You may think it will not benefit you to tell them how to avoid problems because then they won't need you. However, there are plenty of other reasons they can call you. Plus, you will be the person they will turn to any time they need something repaired. In addition, word of mouth goes a long way with customers, and that happy customer may attract you plenty of business.

Adding Value to Your Business

When you are branding, it is important to add value with everything you do. Adding value means making yourself valuable to the customers and the community. This may include giving out free information through tips and tricks, statistics, and other useful bits of information.

You can make the business more

valuable by adding a little extra in everything that you do. A voice mail message might include a quick tip on fixing something or a way to prevent a computer virus. The signature on your email should contain more than your name, address and phone number. You might include a useful sentence underneath that is a quick tip or useful bit of information.

Making yourself useful adds value to your business and to the customers' perception of you. The customers must believe that they need you; this is a part of proving to them you are useful and the best person to turn to when they need something.

Media Consideration

The media is extremely important when branding a business. There are many different outlets and each can be used to your advantage, even for damage control. Proper branding means staying connected with the media. Make the media your friend. Some say to keep your friends close and your enemies closer; this is true with the media. They can make you very popular or they can ruin you. There is really no in-between. You need the media on your side at all times.

Local Media

There are many local media outlets you might consider using when you are looking to brand your company or your products. You can use local newspapers to announce sales and events. The television stations are useful when running advertisements or announcing events on the news.

One thing to keep in mind is that public television stations are free; they cannot charge you money to run something on them. If you are a non-profit organization looking to brand your organization, the best way to do it is through public television stations. You can announce events like blood drives and other events on public television. This is great exposure, and it is free.

Other forms of local media may be local websites for town members. Some towns have a site for the community (such as AmericanTowns.com) where people can post things like classified ads and upcoming events. They are free sites and, because of this, are sometimes used more than the newspapers.

Article Writing

Another way you can use the media to your advantage is to write your own articles and distribute them to the press. This is very beneficial. If the press comes across times they need to fill additional space in their paper, they may use them.

Sending articles to the press is free. They will not charge you to use your articles. If you write useful articles to magazines in the industry in which you work, you may even get paid for the articles. Article writing is a very beneficial way to advertise your business, and it helps with the branding process.

Sponsors

Looking for sponsors is very important. It is very similar to getting an endorsement. You may make a deal with companies to sponsor you; such a deal might include putting up their advertisement at a local event or charity you are holding. You should always look for local or national sponsors. Sponsors can be used on your website and at your business location. The most common way to obtain sponsors is by offering them advertising for their business.

Sponsors need to see a benefit in it for them, and, if they do, they are usually willing to work with you. Finding local sponsors helps you build credibility with your business.

Written Testimonials

Written testimonials are very important in the branding process because they work in two ways. They help build credibility and trust with the targeted audience. When you sell products or services, it is important to gather as many written testimonials from your customers as you can. A customer can write up the type of product or service he purchased from your company and his experience working with you. The more written testimonials you have, the better.

Written testimonials are beneficial because they create hype. They increase the excitement about your business and make people want to try your product. Testimonials tell the public that you followed through on delivering the promise you made. Importantly, this shows you are reliable and consistent. It shows that you deliver.

Special Offers

Building a brand also requires you to provide offers and special discounts to the customers.

Customers are always looking for a great deal, and when they know they can get it from you, they will shop from you. You might offer discount codes to customers for specific items or even a "buy one get one free" deal. These are excellent ways to promote a business. If you have an online company, you may offer free shipping or other types of discounts during specified periods of time.

Special offers work very well with customers. Free items usually work the best because customers find that very little is ever free. Although it is not cost effective to give away free items, you may include something free with a purchase of a bigger item.

Referrals

Another media consideration when you are building up your brand is that you need to work on obtaining referrals. Referrals work very well in building up your brand. Referrals are the word of mouth endorsements from customers who swear by you. These can be difficult to build, but referrals help in establishing your credibility.

You can help with gaining referrals to your business by offering specials or discounts to customers that refer you to other customers.

This may be a $5 discount on their next purchase or something similar. When customers see there is a benefit in it for them, they will often times refer your company to others to gain the benefit. This helps increase a customer base, revenues and brand awareness.

The Competitive Edge

Creating a competitive edge is another important aspect of branding. Today, the online world has many methods of branding. The most popular method of branding and gaining the competitive edge is through the use of blogs.

Blogs allow a site to increase traffic, to improve rank through search engine results and even to help with building credibility.

About Blogs

Blogs are websites that use the new Web 2.0 technology, which allows visitors to a site to post their own comments, articles and feedback. Giving users access to post comments to your site allows them to feel a sense of ownership in your business. Blogs work in many ways, which may include forums and discussion boards, or they sometimes look like a daily diary. They keep visitors up-to-date on current events and allow for discussion to take place.

Reasons to Use Blogs

There are many reasons to use blogs for a business. A business may want to provide a discussion board that allows other customers to discuss troubleshooting tips and tricks. A company may post useful information about how to get the most longevity out of products, how to repair or fix things, and even how to prevent problems.

Using a Blog to Your Benefit

If you decide to add a blog to your company site, there are many things to consider so you get the most out of it. Some companies allow people to post their own content. The content on your blog should include your important keywords and phrases, links, useful product or service information, and contact information.

The primary purpose of blog writing for branding is to gain more exposure for a business and get the word out to people that the company exists. Blogs are an excellent way to create hype and exposure because the web has millions of businesses and customers.

When using a blog, it is essential to make sure that you use important keywords that are relevant to the products and services offered by your business. These keywords and phrases should be the words that will be typed into the search engines when a user is looking for what you offer. The keywords should be used naturally throughout the content of the blog. They will work by allowing your blog to be pulled up in the search engine results when users type in the specific keywords and phrases you used in the blog.

Adding links to blogs is a very important thing for two reasons. They provide an easy method to get back to your site, and they provide an inbound link. Users always appreciate an easy way to get to your company. Talking in a blog about products and services offered without links to where the customers can find them will not be helpful. Customers will only search for a business for a very short time. You have a better chance of getting new customers when a link is right there in the blog so they can easily click on it and find out more about the company.

URLs are also beneficial for a business because they provide inbound links. One of the ways that search engines work is that they rank a business by popularity. Popularity can be built up by links integrated within blogs. The more inbound links you provide in a blog, the more popularity a search engine thinks you have. Never forget to place inbound links inside the content you place on your blog.

A blog needs to provide beneficial information for the visitors and readers. When there is something useful to the readers, they will come back for more. Blogs also give you the opportunity to give free advice and useful information that will benefit users and cause you to gain credibility for being knowledgeable about the products and services offered.

Remember, your brand is represented by your ;

Accomplishments

Values

Passions

Vision

Purpose

"I am a great believer in luck...
The smarter I work, the more I have."
Mark Zupo – 2001

More importantly, instead of "Who do **you** think you are?" the question may be better stated as "Who do **they** think you are?" Who you are is reflected in who you are perceived to be. Your presence is fortified by charisma and is a direct reflection of your character. If your **charisma is genuine,** it is always a reflection of your **character.**

Charisma without Character

If you have charisma without character, it's only a matter of time before people find you out. So what is it about a **strong, honest character** that is so important to charisma? Consider the following truths about character:

-Character Lasts

There was a time when people who lacked integrity stood out from the crowd. Now the opposite is true – charisma can make you stand out for a moment as a "flash in the pan" or "flavor of the week," but character will set you apart for a lifetime.

-Character is Trustworthy

Some people are actually suspicious of charisma. Having good character, however, inspires trust. Couple trust with charisma and you become a force that others want to be around.

-Charismatic Behavior Inspires Character

If you lead people, your good character sets a standard for everyone who is following you. People can't emulate your charisma, but they can aspire to your character. If leaders compromise their standards, cheat the company or take shortcuts, so will their followers. And no amount of charisma can make that situation right.

-Character Toughs It Out

During the rough times, which all leaders face; character has the ability to carry you through, which is something that charisma can never do. When you are weary and inclined to quit, **the self-discipline of character** keeps you going.

-Character Is In It for the Long Haul

Charisma, by its nature, doesn't extend very far. It usually produces a quick, blinding light, but then it's gone. Character, on the other hand, is more like a bonfire. Its effects are long-lasting. It produces warmth and light, and as it continues to burn, it gets hotter, providing fuel that burns brighter.

-Character Makes Things Easier

If you're currently leading people, you probably have some measure of both charisma and character. The question is which one are you relying on to lead? The answer can be found in your response to this great question:

"As time goes by, does it get easier or harder to lead?"

Without character, charisma becomes harder to sustain. You constantly have to entertain to get people to notice you. But with character, your influence strengthens, builds, and continues to attract people over time. And best of all, the ones who do come to enjoy your fire stay with you a lot longer than the ones who only want to see a show.

Reputation Management

An individual's reputation is relative. Your reputation is relative to your actions, your visibility, your influence and your intentions. Your brand is your reputation. A person can have great power and control that is achieved by creative deception. A person can deceive the masses with smooth talk and promises that will never be delivered.

One can be powerful and in command of others due to the *perception* that they are in charge. We can be deceived into believing in the promises of those who appear to be genuine. There is a difference, though, between deception and perception.

"Choose your friends wisely; We are most like the five people we are closest to."
Mark Zupo - 2009

- **Deception:** The intention to deceive, a fraud. A trick or an imposter.

  An imposter who presents himself as though he has authority and credibility is often discovered soon after he commands power and takes control. Sometimes it is too late and the result is at the expense of those around him. These imposters' control is never long lasting or of much value.

- **Perception: 1.** The act or faculty of comprehending by means of the senses or of the mind; cognition; understanding. **2.** Immediate or intuitive recognition or appreciation, as of moral, psychological, or aesthetic qualities; insight; intuition; discernment: *an artist of rare perception.* **3.** The result or product of perceiving, as distinguished from the act of perceiving; percept.

"Every drop of water is just as wet as any other drop of water."
Mark Zupo - 2007

When the people around us have a perception of which we are, we must be forthright with our explanation of which we truly are, what we stand for and what it may mean to others. Our explanation must be clear and precise because it will be a valuable instrument in our tool chest, especially when we represent that we have something that is of value to them.

Notice that the definition of perception contains words like quality, insight, intuition, discernment, appreciation and morals. These are the valuable traits that we deliver when we present ourselves to others to gain their trust and confidence. When people hear my name, what do they think of first? What value do I lend to those around me? Do I have a persona?

Mark Zupo

Chapter 9

The Big Picture

If money is your hope for independence you will never have it. The only real security that a man will have in this world is a reserve of knowledge, experience, and ability.
Henry Ford

Vision

In fact, turning your knowledge into cash is more simple than you think. You have to be very

interested and committed to developing your life product to succeed and then, and only then, will it be relatively easy to draw the clients that will pay you a fortune…all while you work from the comfort of your home!

Simply put, with the right help and direction, you can use a book to start your first Internet-Based Business or promote your existing business enterprises. If your speaking ability is poor then you need the training that comes with experience. It will be the experience you'll get after you have written a book that can catapult you to recognition.

Then you'll be asked to speak!

Being a paid armature or professional speaker will make you money BUT being a professional speaker who sells his or her own products can then be Highly Paid!

. . . Most speakers lose more than they earn

When speakers promote their seminars and speak for profit, they lose more than they earn! That's right. One simple tool and technique I learned from a mentor is worth a Million dollars by itself.

. . . Professionals know the tricks and tips that rake in the money!   *You can, too.*

<u>The first thing you must understand is that you have to treat your life like a business.</u>

To differentiate yourself in this business you must practice the skills that make you a professional. If you don't treat it like a business and dedicate yourself to learning all the things you need to know to be successful, you will fail.

Know Thyself

We meet new people every day, for work or otherwise—whether we interact with them or not, you develops instinctive likes and dislikes towards people. This has lot to do with their personality.

To think that your personality is made up of

only the way you look would be anomalous however. Your ideas, the way you think, your priorities in life, your emotions all comprise your personality. You need to understand and accept yourself the way you are if you want to be happy.

You can take a personality test to help you figure out what kind of personality you have. A substantial number of these are available online and in different books. Think about how much you know yourself. What are the things that are important for you?

Put all societal and familial expectations aside for a minute and think about what you really want to do, what would make you happy? Knowing yourself well is important and will serve you well in various situations.

When you are looking for a job, for example, it would be ideal to not get stuck with something that you don't want to do. Knowing yourself would also help you accept other people as they are. It will help you develop an open mind.

One way or the other, the ultimate thing is to do things that are important for you and that make you happy. If you are an introvert, you should regularly spend quality time by yourself. You can also keep your diary, if you are uncomfortable sharing your deeper thoughts with other people. Don't hesitate to stand by what you believe in.

This is important for you to be happy. It will be good for you to develop a constructive hobby. If you are introvert don't succumb to peer pressure and compulsively spend time with people. Learn how to say no. Draw lines around you and your space as and when you need to.

Extroverts on the other hand should get involved in group activities like theatre for example. Learn new things whenever possible. Don't hesitate to experiment. Stay in regular touch with your friends and family. If you have any introvert friends, learn to accept them as they are.

In your growing up years, a lot of things that are going on around you, go into shaping your personality. Some experts also believe that a lot of genetic factors go into making you who you are. But the important thing is to accept you the way you are. If there are certain things about you that you don't like however, you can try to make minor alterations.

Discover Your Personality?

One of the most significant aspects of the modern world is the way you look and carry you. People are much inclined to appear like the movie stars or models of any fashionable person that they admire.

These famous personalities are considered to be paragons of fashion and beauty. But we always need to keep in mind that beauty is not just about wearing the right dress and looking hip.

The most important factor that fashions beauty is your personality. We hardly look into this factor anymore. Once your personality is refined, you will have mastered eternal beauty. Research reveals that men, often, prefer people who might not be very good looking but are sweet, interactive and trustworthy. Thus this shows that women who are not considered to be conventionally beautiful but have great personalities do attract a lot of attention.

It is not a conflict between personality and good looks. Allow both these aspects in to mature simultaneously and you will notice that your personally will accentuate your good looks and vice versa.

Understand Yourself

The primary thing that you need to do is understand yourself. It is essential for you to comprehend your personality in order to refine it and thus improve your physical beauty. Let the process be slow and gradual.

You can also consult the various books and other content that is available – they will help you locate your character. Opt for the examinations as well as the help teams that are found on the test to know yourself better.

Each Person is Distinct and Special

One person can always consider another person's character and attitude in a negative light. Often people consider hyperactive or unusually quiet people to be crazy or odd. This notion is rather relative- each one appears little strange to another person. You can always utilize your attitude to improve yourself.

Supervising Your Virtues and Vices i.e. Your Features

Sort out your virtues and vices. Be a good person and get rid of all your negative points...

Focus on your virtues. If you wish to make your personality an instrument in order to be more appealing, then surely concentrate on your virtues and let your virtues be the attention centre. Each person is special and distinct in his or her own way. So let the good in you shine in front of others!

Personality is an essential component of the self of a person. By perfecting your personality you will be able to reveal the beauty that lies within you.

Personality is not distinct from your external beauty. It is just an external manifestation of your internal splendor. It is important for you to let people understand that beauty is not just about good looks.

How Law of Attraction Helps in Personal Development

Laws of attraction can be very crucial when you are trying to understand your personality and its development. Failures and successes are a part of life and should be taken in the same spirit.

The ideal thing is to take all your failures as lessons for your life. Take these incidents to understand your limitations and things that you did wrong and try not to repeat them in the future. This is how you can pave the way for your success.

Deal with your failures as and when they occur. To keep them locked inside you and drag those along wherever you go will only complicate your present and future.

What you think is what you are, is one of the most important laws of attraction. If you are always surrounded by negative, pessimistic thoughts it will hamper your growth and personality development.

Given below are some things you need to consider and sought out if you are working towards a positive personality:

Learn you accept yourself the way you are. You might have shortcomings and limitations but so does everybody else. If you can't love yourself, how will you love and accept other people.

No matter how many things are going wrong

around you, learn to take control. The moment start pitying yourself, you have lost half the battle already.

Even if you are surrounded by people who have a lot of negativity don't let it get to you. Try and make them see the brighter side of life if possible. But learn to step away as and when they start getting to you. No matter how messed up things are, tomorrow would be a new day and a new beginning. Stop mulling over your failures and try to fix things the best you can.

It's important to set goals for yourself. But make sure that the goals are realistic. Also reward yourself as and when you achieve desired results.

Learn to be confident about yourself. If you are sure about what you want go ahead and get it. Don't let anything put you down.

Developing your personality means discovering your weaknesses and working on them. Learning from your failures and making sure that you don't commit the same mistakes again and again in crucial.

Learn to be good to yourself and do things that make you happy. If you are good to people then you would *attract the same kind of behavior and people*. Learn to be positive and happy and everything will start to look up.

Do You Have A Positive Attitude?
Take the Quiz

This chapter presents the latest information on positive attitude. It is designed to either reconfirm your knowledge or enhance your knowledge on the subject by routing your thoughts on positive attitude through 5 questions.

1. Am I happy being where I am today?

This is a trick question without any standard answer, but knowing how to deal with it is crucial: for believing that you are happy can actually increase your happiness and contentment, and give you the confidence and positive attitude for anything that you wish to achieve. So do not simply wish to be happy but come out and believe that you really are: enjoy and be thankful for the little things in life and see what a difference it makes.

2. Am I appealing to the opposite sex?

Even if you do not have an answer to this, it shouldn't stop you from doing anything you wish. So be it shaping up, changing your dressing style or hairdo, your attitude towards people or life, do it as if you were appealing, and it shall conduce to your benefit. Remember that what matters the most is how well you can carry it off rather than exactly what you are trying to carry off.

3. How much could I have?

Operative here is not a standard that could define having too much or having too little, but rather how the question of how badly you really need or desire it. This boils down to asking yourself what, and how much, you are willing to work and sacrifice for something you think you want. If you really are willing to sweat for it, then no matter what, work on towards what you have set your heart on and the sky is the limit.

4. What motivates me?

Human desires are endless, and there are infinite variations to the things that make people happy. If you do not know what drives you or sets your pulse racing, approach life like a buffet service. Try everything piece by piece until you locate your favorite dish.

5. What Really Makes You Tick?

Understanding what really makes you tick is to not only be able to define your goal but also the path that you seek to chart towards that goal. So identify what you really want and what you are willing to do for it. It's all about knowing yourself; you own limits and doing your own cost benefit analysis, rather than any very profoundly philosophic quest.

Take Action!

The success (or failure) of your Internet Entrepreneurship really is up to you now. If you succeed, the credit will all belong to you and if you fail, you will own that as well. Your success or failure is in your own hands.

Success and failure are two sides of the same coin. The coin in question is your own Internet Entrepreneurship and you don't want to flip that coin into the air and leave it to chance as to whether it lands on success or failure.

You want complete control over the fate of your Internet business and you do have that control.

Every decision will be yours to make. If you make wise choices then you will claim victory and success will be yours. If you make unwise choices then your internet business will crash and burn and your own hopes and dreams will go up in flames along with it.

You deserve to be RICH!

Chapter 10
Follow the Leader

Do not hire a man who does your work for money, but him who does it for love of it.

Henry David Thoreau

"Making money is an art, and the value of art is in the eye of the beholder"

- Mark Zupo

Process 1-2-3™

1. **The First Step** in the process is to have a means for people to find you. In this ever-changing world of technology, it is more important for people to find you in the easiest, fastest and most efficient way possible...via the Internet.

<u>**You must have a webpage that is the domain of your name.**</u>

Specifically, like mine, http://www.MarkZupo.com. Check out my main website and see what I mean. It is all about me and what I do. You can and should have your own website in your name as well.

Make Money from Your Website…………….

2. **The Second Step** in the process is to have a product or products to sell. Products that specifically are yours and no-one else's. Products that define who you are, what you're about or what you represent to anyone else. After all, who best to tell people about you than you? Who knows you better than you?

-If You Have a Speech...

If you have ever been to a presentation at a convention center, a hotel meeting room, or a social function, you have heard someone speak about a topic that usually seeks to separate you from your money. However the topic isn't the important issue here...the presentation is.

When you listened to some person speak, you might have said to yourself, "I could have done that!" The speaker was poor, the speech was poor and the message was even worse.

The presentation skills of the speaker left a lot to be desired and you certainly could have done just as good or even better, right?

The point is, given the same opportunity, you can do the same presentation, even better with some guidance and a little professional help. The real point is you can be paid handsomely for it, as well.

Everyone has an opinion about something. People who voice their opinions are heard, liked or disliked based on how the messages are received and the intents are perceived. The one difference separating you from those of authority and credibility is visibility.

Someone who has written a book is automatically perceived to be an authority just because they wrote a book...any book about any topic! The easiest way to write a book is to write on a topic that is dear to you, a passion, or something you know a great deal about.

<u>Presto...you have just become a member of an elite group of authors!</u>

You are now recognized as a credible source of information and an authoritative source because...you said so!

When Mohammed Ali was asked, "Why did he think he was the world's greatest boxer?" He replied, "Because...I said so!"

Your first assignment is to write a book. There is a book in everyone.

There are huge benefits to writing a book.

> **Just about every famous person you have ever heard of either became famous because they wrote a book or they became more famous because they wrote a book.**

Just pick a name of someone you know that is famous and see what the title of their book is because I am sure they have one. It doesn't matter what industry, walk of life, subject, political, religious, social or business area in life, a book has been written on it by someone who has made money on it.

A book makes you an expert. It makes you an authority. A book establishes you as a credible source. There is no other medium that can deliver the results that writing a book can.

Your book makes you stand out in a world of experts because you are an authority in your industry or area of expertise. Some examples are;

- Robert Kiyosaki – Rich Dad Poor Dad
    Virtually unknown until he wrote a book.
- Brendon Burchard – Life's Golden Ticket
    Virtually unknown until he wrote a book.
- Tom Clancy – The Hunt for Red October
    Virtually unknown until he wrote a book.
- Timothy Ferriss – The Four Hour Work Week
    Virtually unknown until he wrote a book.

A book could blast you to notoriety, fame and fortune with a mere mention of your book on the right media platform like CNN, Oprah and the like. Once you get noticed, your name and business will take on a life of its own.

Your book is;

- ✓ A Tool to be Recognized
- ✓ A Door Opener
- ✓ A Business Card
- ✓ A Method to Charge More Based on Perception
- ✓ A Device to Generate Revenue
- ✓ A Means to Develop Multiple Streams of Income

The Third Step

Build a database (list) of followers and customers.

Develop Your Database (List)

A database is a list of people that follow you on social media websites like Twitter, Facebook, LinkedIn, YouTube, Blogs, and so on. You can develop a database by offering a free informational product in exchange for an email address.

This may well be the most important step in the process of selling you as a product. This strategy works very well and great attention should be paid to the steps to get the maximum outcome from it.

Aligning yourself with an already respected marketer or easily recognized authority gives the impression of credibility based on your association with your new associate. This authority or celebrity in the business world may also have an established list of their own that can be "rented" to you in exchange for some consideration. You can see evidence of this with Taco Bell and Kentucky Fried Chicken restaurants in the same building.

There can be a shared promotion opportunity between you and another recognized person or company. The association gives an implied endorsement of you and your products.

Once you have focused on a market to direct your campaign and developed a product to sell, you then begin to collect partners in this process who are willing to promote you. Then you establish their list for marketing to for shared exposure or profit. When your new partners help drive traffic to you, you establish and maintain the new list of patrons from that point on.

Any new interested opt-ins to your list and products is seeking to satisfy their own curiosity if they are motivated to. Some will stay and some will go. If you deliver great content, products, or services, you will get great things in return. Here are 7-simple steps to successfully building and monetizing a list:

1. **Specifically define your target market**
   Define who you are selling to with precision and specificity

2. **Create an irresistible lead generating magnet**
   Get their attention and deliver unbelievable value

3. **Create an email marketing campaign**
   Capture and store permission-based opt-ins

4. **Convert your new leads from an opt-in squeeze page**
   Publish a squeeze page that hits hard and demands action

5. **Drive traffic to your opt-in page with social media**
   Use social media in every form to direct attention to your site

6. **Instill sincerity and trust in your new list of opt-ins**
   Build trust, establish credibility, and maintain authority and respect

7. **Monetize your list with front and back-end sales**
   Solve problems, create, promote and sell what people want, offer more, offer it again

The point of establishing your own list is to market to them forever. Let's do some simple math to establish just how important everyone is to you. For every subscriber you have collected that pays you $10 dollars, it will add up to thousands very quickly.

> **"If you think you can,
> Or you think you can't,
> either way you're right!"**
>
> **Henry Ford**

Chapter 11

Passion Power, Persistence, Prosperity

> To give real service you must add something which cannot be bought or measured with money, and that is sincerity and integrity.
>
> - Douglas Adams

The First Lesson: Mindset

In this life of technology, impersonal modes of communication, corporate indoctrination and cultural diversity, a person can be overwhelmed with an identity crisis. Who am I? What do I do? Why do I do it? For whom am I doing it? What is my real value? What am I really worth...and to whom?

You can see that your mindset is as crucial as any other aspect of the process to define who you are and what you can contribute, especially what you can contribute that will make you money! These characteristics are borne from the duty of all men and women, and they become the lasting impression of who you are. They are also the business of your life. They are the business of your experiences that you can profit from if you know how.

- Adversity Builds Character…….and **experience**.
- Responsibility Builds Respect…and **confidence**.
- Accountability Builds Honor……and **ethics**.
- Privilege Builds Humility…………and **trust**.
- Dependability Builds Trust………and **credibility**.

    A number of people have passed through my life. Some did good things and some did not. I have great admiration and respect for those who touched my life in a positive way; I learned great lessons from them. One such person was my Uncle Ed. Uncle Ed was a big guy. It was obvious to me that he had strength and power, but he was as gentle as a lamb. It didn't matter when I had an opportunity to speak to him, whether it was casually, by design or just because I was wasting time, I learned a great deal from everything he had to say.

Ok...I know now that he was talking to a kid and that he tempered his comments to fit my age, but it didn't matter because the insight, motivation and lessons he gave were just as valuable then as they are today.

-You deserve to be Rich!

My Uncle Ed was a kind and good man whose gentle ways were often mistaken for weakness. On the contrary, Uncle Ed was a strong and dutiful man with a great power of influence and with an enviably dynamic vision.

Once, I had the opportunity to stay with him for a few weeks, which gave me many opportunities to talk to him "man to man." Having the foresight of a dreamer and achiever-to-be, I asked him, "What will the future bring for me? Will I be rich?" He answered as only Uncle Ed could answer, **"Markey-Boy, you deserve to be rich!"**

That was all I needed to hear. It was the license I needed to achieve my goals of wealth and freedom. I was able to visualize my future right there and then. The best thing about that vision is that I saw I would earn a living from doing the things I love, instead of from working for someone else as I helped to make him or her rich. It didn't take college to teach me that; it just took working the farm.

-The more I have...the happier I'll be

When you grow up on a real working farm, you have little and you have much. When you try to calculate the value of your material items, it appears you have very little. When you perceive what you have in the sense of opportunity, life experience and blessing, it adds up to unbelievable fortune.

One misconception that I had while growing up on the farm was that "If I had more I would be happier." Not so. I learned this only after amassing a fortune for the second time in my life and losing it all - again. After losing a million dollar fortune for the second time, I was actually somewhat relieved to be without all that money again. There was relief from the pressure of how to invest it, when to sell stocks, who might try to steal it and who would fight over it after I was gone.

Who would have ever thought that I would earn more than a million dollars in my life...let alone that I would do it twice? And who would ever have thought that I could lose it twice as well? As smart as I thought I was and as smart as other people thought I was, I failed to invest in my future properly to protect my legacy.

My future successes have been determined by my commitment to succeed. I have never lost that passion, and I live by its credo every day of my life.

"Commitment is what transforms a promise into reality."
Mark Zupo – 2007

-Future Achievement is a Poor Plan

Having amassed a fortune before I was thirty years old was, in itself, a banner achievement for a kid. At twenty-five, I was worth a million dollars. Actually, I was worth more than a million dollars...but who's counting?

Earning that kind of money seemed easy because the timing was right, the economics were right and, more importantly, no one told me that I couldn't do it! My greatest success came when a man, who we will not name here for legal reasons as he went to prison for fraud and embezzlement, talked me into a real estate investment venture. As luck would have it, I came up with the money to invest; and I bought, on his suggestion, a share of a condominium.

Three days later, a mysterious fire claimed the condominium, which was located in a famous ski resort town. I collected the insurance money for my share of the appraised value of the condo, which equaled three times what I had invested. I made **forty-thousand dollars** on a **five thousand dollar** investment in a weekend! The investment was legal and I was hooked.

Knowing what to do with the money was mystifying. I seemed to have the skills to make money but lacked the skills to keep it for any length of time. The spoils of opportunity for me were also the curse of my accomplishments.

I learned how to spend like I was a millionaire simply because I was. I turned that money into other real estate investments that never seemed to lose money. Every investment I made turned out to be a gold mine. It seemed like I couldn't lose. What I didn't learn, however, was that I needed an education…a business education.

Over the next ten years I went on to

buy condominiums, single family homes, townhouses, duplexes, strip malls and a food franchise. Thinking I was well off in my own right led me to think that I didn't need a college degree; I had earned my right as an entrepreneur by collecting money! I would be wrong again.

What I would have learned if I had attended college were lessons in running my life like a business, necessary lessons if I were to be the head of a household, to have a family and to provide for them a good life of less hardship and toil than I had experienced to this point. I failed to plan!

"Today's mess – tomorrow's success."
Mark Zupo - 2003

-Success Doesn't Bring Happiness...Happiness Brings Success

A valuable lesson I had to learn was what I call "The Lesson of the Wealthy." To be more specific, it was how to be wealthy, which in turn meant how to keep the wealth I made. This is valuable because I seemed happier when I had money than when I did not. No surprise there.

What I discovered was that it was my family who made me happy, not my money. Lose a child to a drunk driver, lose a wife to cancer, lose everything you have ever earned to the economy, and you learn hard lessons in humility, respect, dignity and…happiness.

-Baptism by Fire

"You can't have a message until you've had a mess. You can't have a testimony until you've had a test."

- **Unknown**

I am not sure from where the term "Baptism by Fire" comes, but I assume it means that one's understanding is defined by the end result of an intense experience. This is how I gained some valuable insights into how I should reflect before I say what I'm thinking!

What the Nay-Sayers Say:

- Those who say, **"I wouldn't"** really mean, "I would if the circumstances were safer."

- Those who say, **"I shouldn't"** really mean, "I should when I feel more comfortable about my confidence."

- Those who say, **"I couldn't"** really mean, "I could if I were more secure in my decision-making and risk-taking abilities."

- Those who say anything less than **"I WILL"** may never succeed without taking action!

When I say I wouldn't, shouldn't or couldn't, it is usually because I am fearful about proceeding to act. In fact, however, I never fail to act because I am less afraid of action than I am of what people will think of my failures.

The Second Lesson: Commitment

-Passion Delivers Purpose

There are three principles of absolute accomplishment: Vision, Focus and Action. These three principles are the foundation for achievement, regardless of one's intention, direction or motivation.

- **Vision = Success**

Any goal you have is a product of your vision- in the idea stage, in the formulation stage or in the development stage. Regardless, your vision keeps your focus on the results rather than on the path.

- **Focus = Direction**

Your focus to achieve the end result of your vision is the guide that leads you and keeps you on track. Your focus is your direction and the force that compels you to move forward without distraction.

- **Action = Results**

The action you take is the force that drives you to achievement at every level of your battle. Your action at any level delivers results at every level. If you maintain your vision, preserve your focus and take action, your success will never be diminished by a lack of results.

> *"Power with purpose, purpose with power."*
> **Mark Zupo – 2010**

Your vision, focus and action will

- **Change Lives**
- **Empower People**
- **Lead People**
- **Create Independence**
- **Turn Adversity into Triumph**

The Third Lesson:

5 Principles of Success

1. **Focus on the desired results.**

Make a plan and follow it to the letter. Never give up. Always follow through with it, from the first detail to the last detail. Have **PASSION!**

2. **Develop your situational awareness.**

Learn to recognize problems and obstacles that will come up. Be ready for them. Have a plan of attack to fix them. Be aware of potential risks; accept that they exist and are waiting for you to resolve them immediately. Have **NO FEAR!**

3. **Increase mental flexibility.**

The state of your mind is a state of mind! Control it, manage it, and use it to your advantage. Be sharp; educate yourself. Exercise your functional obedience to your plan, your vision and your focus. Have **PERSISTANCE!**

4. **Maintain mental excellence.**

Develop a routine for stretching your mind and body to maintain sharpness and acute abilities. Exercise your mind and body regularly. No-one can make you a success but you! Have **PERSPIRATION!**

5. **Take action!**

Remember, "Ignorance on fire always beats knowledge on ice!" Action...Action...Action. Those who start and finish what they start are the successful few. They are the winners, the champions, the conquerors, the victors and most importantly...the rich! Have **PURPOSE!**

-Make Your Business...YOUR BUSINESS!

    Entrepreneurship is natural and instinctive. It is innate in every one of us. Entrepreneurship, from the earliest history of man, is a natural method of survival, which we use every day in some form or another. We sell ourselves to our boss and our friends; we sell ourselves to our spouse, our peers, and our clients. We desire to be admired every day. Turning that into income is easier than you think. We simply have to channel that desire for admiration into an income-producing vehicle.

    When we attach capitalism to entrepreneurship, we get income from our efforts. We can get paid to be who we are by people who admire who we are for what we do or for what we have accomplished. This isn't being arrogant or conceited, but rather it is using our talents to capitalize on our strengths and accomplishments. Have you ever read an autobiography? Have you ever purchased a book or audio-CD from someone who has done something that you would like to do?

> ***"Once the mind of man is expanded to the dimensions of new thought, it never retracts to its original size or shape."***
> **Oliver Wendell Holmes, Jr.**

Taking advantage of our ability to convey what we know into a product is what we want to achieve. It is **The Business of YOU™.** The business of you results in the freedom, success and profit you want. Understanding the net value of money delivers the freedom that is your ultimate goal. When you understand this concept, you are well on your way to achieving the success.

If you know what you want, if you know how to get what you want and if you know what you would do to get it, then you have the tools that will lead you to act on your vision and achieve your goals.

The NET Value of money:

- Gets you what you want.
- Drives you to success.
- Forms desire to acquire it.
- Determines what you would do to get it.
- Establishes what you can do for other people too!

Later in this book, we'll discuss how you will take what you have learned throughout your life and turn it into a product that you can rely on forever. The reason this will work: it is all about you.

Who better than you to capitalize on what you have spent your lifetime learning? Now is the time to use what you have learned for your benefit.

There are a few methods that will help you skyrocket your visibility and recognition as an authority or an expert in your field or your niche. Once you have seen the process, you'll be well on your way to changing your life!

"Your actions at any level deliver results at every level."

Mark Zupo – 2010

Chapter 12
The Power to Prosper

**When I chased after money, I never had enough. When I got my life on purpose and focused on giving of myself and everything that arrived into my life, then I was prosperous.
Wayne Dyer**

. . . It is really sad... but. . .

Most of the people that try to become professional speakers lose their shirt and some more...mostly because they don't listen.

- They don't follow success.
- They don't copy success.
- They don't have a mentor.

<u>Proper training and guidance is an absolute necessary evil.</u>

<u>This could be the day your life changes!</u>

I've always thought my life was worth more than the life insurance I carried on it. In fact, I believe in my heart that my life is worth more than all of the gold in Fort Knox because my life is and will be self-sustaining and as everlasting that I can make it.

As long as my children continue to remember me they will have the ability to capitalize on my life just like Elvis's family has made more on his fame after his demise than he ever did while he was alive.

I knew I was worth much more than anyone in corporate America was willing to pay me. That, my friends, is unacceptable. It is unacceptable for me and it is unacceptable for you.

Your attitude about your self-worth is directly related to your income and it will fluctuate in parallel at every instance of your wavering or teetering in either direction.

What you learned in school has had the greatest effect on what you believe your self-worth to be and has done a great disservice to every American.

-The Business of Your Life

As a young man, I was always blessed by the belief that

<u>I deserve to be Rich.</u>

Mark Zupo

The Right Mindset for Success

Unfortunately, so many people think that they can quit their jobs, open an internet business and just relax and enjoy life. They expect instant success and instant wealth without having to invest anything (even time and effort) to affect that success.

They really believe that they can sleep until noon, work when and if they want to and just rack up sales and profit. This attitude probably accounts for at least half of all of the failures of new internet businesses.

Making an internet business successful takes a lot of time and even more work. That old real world job demanded that you be on the job for probably 40 hours each week.

Your net internet business will need about twice that many hours each week if it is to become successful. Very, very, very few people are willing to invest that much time and effort thus the 90% failure rate. Of the few that are willing to put in enough time and effort most expect instant success.

They don't even consider the fact that they will need to continue to meet their own personal expenses for many months before they see the first penny of profit from a new internet business even though those facts are readily available.

These are the ones who go out there looking for get-rich-quick schemes and end up becoming victims of internet scam artists.

The right mindset is this: You must expect to work hard. You must expect to work long and tedious hours. You will not be an over-night success. People are not going to line up to give you their money. You are going to have to earn it.

Your Business Success Depends on your Positive Attitude

Your business will prosper greatly if you build and consequently sustain a positive attitude. Even when things in your business are not going according to plan, you have to remember that you are not alone. All business ventures have their ups and downs.

Those impediments can be easily overcome and you can always get back on track if you keep a positive outlook to everything. You will also have increased confidence in yourself and your business capabilities.

A positive attitude will make finding prospective customers simpler. Others will react well to your optimism. They will want to hire you and suggest you to others.

This will also assist you in other departments of life. You will be in good health. Positive people have less fear of heart inflictions.

Mark Zupo

Here are some useful tips for you to expand on your positive attitude.

- **Be Nice to Others:** Being polite and friendly with other individuals will make you feel nice about yourself. You will have a brilliant and happy day. However, you shouldn't be gullible and allow people to manipulate you because of your friendliness.

- **Mix with Other Positive People and Avoid Those who Have Negative Attitudes:** Attitudes rub on to others very quickly. If you spend more of your time with positive people you will automatically find yourself developing a more optimistic attitude.

   However, negative attitudes can also be very infectious.

   There is a popular saying which goes, "Misery loves company". When you are always in the company of people who perpetually complain, you will automatically find yourself beginning to do the same. Insignificant factors that would normally not bother you will suddenly seem to spoil your entire day. You will feel like you have lost all your energy.

   The moment you lose enthusiasm and incentive, it can prove very difficult to get back on track. These factors can take a negative toll on your business. You will not get anything constructive done this way.

- **Be Organized and Practice Time Management:** When you are systematic you will work faster and be able to complete more tasks. You will know exactly what you need to do achieve your target each day. You will do constructive work if you stay within a system instead wasting time searching for phone numbers or email addresses that you have misplaced.

- **Be Proactive:** The moment you are aware of an oncoming obstacle in your work, solve it instead of leaving it till the last instant. Be practical and have a solution ready before the problem can get out of hand. By being ahead of possible impediments, you will permanently be able to avoid setbacks.

- **Consider Hiring a Coach:** Many individuals hire tutors nowadays to attain success in business. These tutors of guides will assist you in deciding exactly what you require your business to yield. They will set attainable targets and will also demand justifications for actions.

Therefore, the right and positive attitude is the most important ingredient for a successful business. Practice it as well as follow it daily.

You'll soon see you have become much more successful than you ever conceived of.

How You Can Master Success

The thing about starting a business…any business…..is that there is no guarantee of success under any circumstances.

Even big international businesses can fail at new business ventures. Failure is always an option but the possibility of success can be optimized.

You can optimize the possibility of success by:

1. **Having a good solid business plan in place BEFORE you launch your online business.** There is an old saying: "Those who fail to plan, plan to fail". A detailed set of plans for success needs to be made. You need to have the steps from getting from point A to point B listed in great detail that include realistic cost estimates for accomplishing each step.

2. **Expecting to work very hard to accomplish your goals.** You must never expect anything to be easy. You will be right most of the time because things are rarely as easy as they look. Each step toward success requires work, time and patience. Sometimes things don't work out right on the first try.

You have to be willing to try again and again until you do succeed.

3. **Not falling for 'get-rich-quick schemes.**
   The internet woods are full of those who prey upon those who are looking for quick and easy ways to become rich. Those ways do not exist. Get over thinking that there is an easy way. There is NOT.

Remember those statistics! Ninety percent of all new internet businesses fail in the first 120 days. You don't have to be part of that majority. You can become a part of that 10% minority of successful internet business enterprises.

Develop the Ideal Personality for Success in Business

A few days back when my associate informed me about this fresh advertising organization and also acquainted me with their webpage, I immediately looked into it. Well, it was absolutely detestable!

It definitely had pretty pictures and a flashy look but the write up could hardly be read or understood. The webpage was designed craftily but was not a user friendly webpage.

The webpage was pathetic as it lacked a unique personality. It had no distinctive feature or that zing to hold my attention. The write up was quite uninteresting and so were the apparently lovely pictures. The write-up consisted of too many We's! The website lacked vitality and enthusiasm. It was a bit too perfect in its endeavor to impress all and thus could impress none!

People generally wish to conduct trade with people they have faith in and are fond of. You need to understand that people will be fond of you only

when your personality impresses them. There is no use at all concealing your true personality behind the veil of that silly, dull and dreary website! People will never get to be acquainted with you this way and they will also not wait for you for too long.

According to Dan Kennedy, if you are dull and tedious in your advertising plans then it will lead you absolutely nowhere. No one will bother to pay you any attention if you are uninteresting. Most people will not even turn to look twice- there is so much more to do in life and so many other interesting things to look into!

Well these questions are now forming clouds in your mind: how will I work things out in case am not appreciated or in case I put off potential buyers? Well this might be the case with you and it probably should too. I shall explain why I incorporate the word "SHOULD".

The moment you are writing a note that is so sugar coated, you should immediately realize that it will be extremely dull and will attract none. In your endeavor to make it appealing, you will actually put off people. Your note will not incite any enthusiasm and hence you will not receive any clients. They would prefer someone who is adequately interesting.

Peter Montoya says that a nice label can excite people and also similarly fend them off. Hence if your organization is not resisting a certain crowd, then it is also not attracting your potential customers in a way it should.

Deter those people who would not be attracted to your personality or your commodities generally and yet wish to conduct business with you. Fend them off right from the start because they will never be fond of someone of your personality or be satisfied with your merchandise. It will never be a good deal!

Business is not just about formalities and official statements. This is the conventional view about business. You might be little apprehensive in the beginning but know that the more thrilling and stimulating your web content as well as write up is, the more popular will be the response to it.

So you understand that your personality needs to blend in your label. Here you ask yourself "how do I go about this?" Well you will have to wait awhile- look into your inbox! I shall be giving you certain hints and suggestions in the upcoming copy.

Maintaining Positive Attitude

Successful people are identifiable by their masterful positive attitude, which makes it appear as if there's nothing that they couldn't achieve if they wanted and nothing they couldn't possess! It is a positive attitude which separates the successful from the losers: a self realized energy that propels towards success as opposed to a self defeating one that creates problems and provokes suffering in life.

Positive attitude is a state and condition of your mind that allows you to handle stress with optimism and patience, promoting hope and nullifying despair. This empowers you to be undeterred by problems, maintain your focus and continue to persevere without frustration, and thus eventually overcome all problems.

So if you have been a pessimist and have been filled with negative thoughts, here's how to get rid of your problem, embrace your cherished goals and develop a positive attitude.

1. **When you sense any signs of negativity or pessimism creeping into your mind, immediately check your thoughts and stop:** Instead try to imagine and visualize your favorite memories, expectations or ideals.

2. **Experts recommend another way to banish negative thoughts from your**

mind, a mechanism which involves two basic stages: The first which drives away negative thoughts and emotions, and the second which allows negativity to be infiltrated and overcome with positive thoughts and feelings.

3. **Talking to you and repeating positive affirmations are proven techniques to develop a positive mindset.** So devise your personal prep talk and motivation statement and make it a point to talk to yourself regularly.

4. **Another helpful way is to make posters or sticky notes carrying positive and affirmative statements such as: I can do it, Success is mine, My goal is within reach, etc, and to put them up around your home or workplace where you are apt see the message regularly, day and night.**

5. **Try to make the highly successful people be your friends and acquaintances, and try and spend time with them and know their approach.** In the right company, it's easy for the secret to a positive attitude to rub off onto you.

6. **Begin to read positive self help books and magazine, or better still the biographies or autobiographies of your heroes.** You could also attend relevant seminars and workshops.

Remember that a positive attitude can only be cultivated and maintained by you; it is wholly internal to you which nobody can take away. It requires much time, effort and dedication, but is an invaluable asset.

Maintain a Positive Attitude During Hard Times

Often there are times when everything seems to go wrong despite one's hardest efforts. During these times, a positive attitude will assist a person to regain his stamina and come out of the rough patch easily.

You should never blame yourself for things that naturally seem to go wrong in life. These incidents cannot be avoided. You should always remember that tomorrow brings the hope of a new day.

Most days turn out to be positive for people, but there will always be occasional pitfalls when nothing seems to go right. Just take the failed day in your stride and move on ahead with the assurance that a better day will soon come.

Always let go of the distress of today and keep faith in the anticipation that tomorrow brings. Most of the days in an individual's life bring about positive results. If you can maintain a positive attitude regardless of what might happen, the bad days will be kept to a bare minimum.

Always remember that a positive attitude will help you recover quicker in times of distress. Some bad days will motivate you to have an even more positive attitude so that you can learn from the mistakes of today for a better tomorrow.

The situation may be extremely difficult. But a positive attitude will help you overcome irrespective of how bad the situation is and you will definitely regain your confidence and self respect.

Hard times will always appear in life. But they seem less hard when life is viewed optimistically. No matter how a hard life may seem at some stage, a positive attitude will help you keep your head clear and allow you to think steadily so that you can find the right solution.

Even at work, a positive attitude will help you keep your calm and you will be able to do all the tasks that need to be done to improve the situation. You will be able to end your day on an optimistic note.

Even when you are sick or in despair, a positive attitude will help you recover quicker. The illness or the disappointment will pass sooner. You should not break down simply because you don't feel fit and fine. Real strength and stamina come from learning to be optimistic and believing that time will soon change for the better.

No one is flawless. Making mistakes is a natural part of life. You have to learn from your wrongdoings and be prepared for the future. You should not always blame yourself and lose your composure when something goes wrong.

Make this a positive learning opportunity for the future. It is easy to maintain a positive attitude during smooth times. It is only when you can do the same during rougher times that you can achieve happiness and success much faster.

Using Your Attitude As Your Ally

It may seem easy to just make your attitude your ally. You probably will not need a lot of convincing to at least give it a try. What do you have to lose? If you are used to letting your attitude lead you, then it is something you are already familiar with.

People make their attitude their ally all the time. Most of the time they do it without even realizing it. Unfortunately, most of the time the attitude is a negative one.

It is often easier to see how a negative attitude acts as an ally than how a positive attitude acts as an ally. This is just human nature to see negative over positive. We are more often drawn to drawing out the negative over the positive. Pessimistic attitudes seem to flood the world, while optimism is slowly drowning.

You can probably come up with many examples of how negative thinking or a negative attitude has turned into a negative situation. You can probably point out negative people and give plenty of examples how that negative attitude is influencing their life.

You may even be able to look at your own life and see how negativity has affected you. It's likely you have let a negative attitude direct you in at least one situation in your life.

Can you remember a time when your negative attitude caused problems in a situation? You can probably look at it now and see just how the negative attitude worked against you. Even if the situation was not a positive one to begin with, your negative attitude likely comes into play.

While this can teach you about how your attitude can become your ally, it also teaches you that you want to do everything possible to make sure your attitude is positive.

If you really want to make your attitude your

ally and you want that ally to be positive, then you need to start looking at the positive. You have to train your mind to find the positive in everything.

You have to ignore the negative. Take the negative you cannot ignore and turn it into a positive. Your ally does not need to be crowded with negativity.

Imagine your ally. An ally filled with negativity is crowded. There are road blocks and other things that get in your way or cause you to not be able to walk the path you choose. You may even have to work to get around these negative things.

If your ally is positive, then it is filled with positive things. There are no roadblocks that you cannot handle. Anything that falls in your way is easy to get past. With an ally filled with positive things you will find that it is easy to travel and that you can get past anything that may come into your path.

You can clearly see that a positive attitude is much better than a negative attitude. You would, obviously, rather have an ally that is easy to get down, than one filled with things that get in your way and slow you down.

Using your attitude as your ally involves many levels of changing your life. You will have to change things you daily, through your interactions with other people, your thoughts and your goals.

As mentioned, the way you shape your thoughts and goals will go a long way towards helping you shape your attitude and making your attitude your ally. Make sure you make a conscious effort to keep these things positive.

When you interact with other people you are basically broadcasting your attitude. You want this to always be positive. People will react to you in a positive manner if you approach them in a positive manner. Your interaction with others is very important in your life.

You want those interactions to be positive. This will allow you to bring positive things into your life. A good example is during a job interview. If you approach the interview with a negative attitude then you likely will not get the job.

Go to the same interview with a positive attitude and you have a better chance of getting that job. The way you approach others can have a huge impact on your life, so make sure you are using your attitude as your ally when interacting with others.

Your attitude should be your ally every day. It will take some time to make it routine. In the beginning, you will likely have to work hard to make sure you are being positive in every aspect of your life. You will have to make an effort to stay positive and to think positive. It can be difficult, especially if you often give in to negative thoughts and actions.

It is also common when you approach a situation in a positive manner that you end up having a positive experience. People are more likely to help you and to go out of their way to make sure you get what you need when you approach things in a positive manner. So with your attitude as your ally, you are opening yourself up to a lot of positive experiences.

Using your attitude as your ally is about making everything in your life positive. That means associating with positive people, keeping yourself in positive situations and surrounding yourself with positive things.

You have to get rid of negativity. You have to start being positive about everything. By doing this, you are creating your ally. You are paving your road with the positive and this will lead you to positive results.

Chapter 13
Intention, Attention, No Tension

Instead of giving money to found colleges to promote learning, why don't they pass a constitutional amendment prohibiting anybody from learning anything? If it works as good as the Prohibition one did, why, in five years we would have the smartest race of people on earth.
Will Rogers

My job #1 is to get you the information you need to be successful…the secrets, which is the foundation for all you'll do as a public figure.

Many prestigious university business techniques ruin the newest MBA graduates from a successful entrepreneurial business life because:

1. They teach people that business is tough.
2. They teach that you have to be special to be a businessperson.
3. They teach people that they can only earn small amounts for large amounts of work.
4. They teach people that they must work and get paid once for it.

"They teach a formula for FAILURE in the true business world!"

My job #2 is to tell you the biggest secrets that are worth a fortune and that you won't find in any university textbook. My job is to tell you what topics are the best sellers. They are the ones that will make you a sought-after speaker and authority to drive the kind of income you deserve.

What you have to learn are the most effective topics and procedures which can make YOU an **effective, energetic and high-impact product.**

There are many benefits to being a public speaker…some unbelievable benefits! One I really like is to travel. I love to travel. I love to cruise to Alaska, Europe, the Mediterranean Sea, Italy, Greece, Japan, China, and New Zealand! My wife and I recently returned from  New Zealand. We flew first class, (the only way I fly now), to Queenstown, (on the southern island). It was the most spectacular trip of our lifetime.

The total cost was over $10,000 dollars!

The speaking event paid $10,000 dollars for one hour and made over $9,000 in product sales!! **"That's right, a total of $19,000 dollars for a "working" vacation."**

We stayed another ten days and visited every place you can think of on both islands. Can you believe it?

Think you can handle that? I'll bet you could get used to being treated like a king. Some of the benefits of public speaking are remarkable. <u>I could not have been so successful without the necessary training and information in advance of trying it out on my own.</u>

You must know what to do before you start out on your own.

Knowing what to do and when to do it is the key to your success.

You have to be prepared for the worst before it happens to be successful in order to sound and become a visible professional.

The Key to Continuous Growth and Expansion

Grow or die! This is one of the laws of nature that applies to all living things. All business lives by this law as well. A business cannot begin, grow to a certain point and then simply remain at that point and continue to thrive.

Growth and expansion are necessary for the business to survive and if that growth and expansion do not happen then the business will fade and die or crash and burn.

Growth and expansion of business must be controlled by the business owners or managers. If growth is too slow, the business lags behind the competition. If growth is too fast, the business can easily become over extended.

A steady controlled growth is the ideal. Of course, the ideal and the reality are sometimes two very different things.

Sometimes the terms 'growth and expansion' are a bit misunderstood. The most obvious meaning of both terms is to get bigger and broader but those meanings are not the only ones that apply.

Growth, for example, can mean gaining knowledge and becoming wiser and expansion can mean broadening the knowledge base from which a company operates.

A small internet based company does not have to grow and expand until it becomes a giant multi-national company in order to survive but the owners and managers of these internet businesses do have to grow by getting smarter and expand by welcoming change with open arms.

Nothing ever just stays the same. Change is the only certainty in the world. What was hot or what worked yesterday is old news today and it will be ancient history tomorrow.

Companies and company owners and managers must grow with and adapt to changes as they happen and on the internet changes happen a lot faster than they do out in the brick and mortar world.

We all agree that growing, adapting and expanding is vital to the survival of any business and maybe especially to Internet business. So the question is: What is the key to growth and expansion of internet based businesses?

When brick and mortar businesses grow and expand, they build bigger buildings and hire more employees but that isn't exactly an option for an internet based business.

The key to growth and expansion of an internet based business is for the business owner or manager to always and continuously invest in them.

They must be willing to stay on the cutting edge of technology and they must be willing to accept and adapt to changes as they occur.

Internet businesses are not buildings. Internet businesses are people. An internet business cannot grow by investing in a larger building. It only grows when the person who is driving that business invests in his or her own knowledge and ability. An internet business cannot expand by investing in hiring more people. An internet business expands when the person who is driving it invests in himself or herself.

The bottom line is this: The key to continuous

growth and expansion of an internet based business is continuous investments being made in the owner or manager of the business. The short answer:

Invest in Yourself

You have no doubt heard this refrain many times. But what does 'invest in yourself mean'? Does it mean you should go out and invest in a haircut that costs two hundred bucks? Does it mean that you should go by yourself a designer suit? What does it mean to invest in yourself?

Well, if you can afford it, go get that haircut and buy that designer suit but that is not the kind of investment that we are talking about here.

Your internet business is just you, your computer and your internet connection and you could actually operate your internet business from any commuter on the planet that had an internet connection.

So basically, your business is really only you. Your business is based only upon your own knowledge and your own ability. Those are the 'company' assets and those are the ones that need to grow and expand constantly so that your internet business thrives.

Here is a rule that you might want to live by to insure that your internet business is a success and continues to be a success: Invest 5% of your time and income into improving yourself.

Expansion and growth are imperative to survival and expansion and growth of an internet business means expanding and growing the knowledge of the person running the company...that would be YOU.

A tiny investment of only 5% of your time and your income per year in yourself can mean that you will continue to see positive monetary returns for many, many years to come. You might be sitting there shaking your head and still wondering what is meant by a 5% time and income investment per year in yourself. What is meant is that you must expand your knowledge.

You must stay on top of new technological advancements and you must expand your knowledge base about your own area of expertise. Things change fast. New information becomes available on almost everything under the sun every day of the week.

It is very, very easy to fall behind very, very quickly. And unless you consciously put forth the effort to stay on top of things you will most certainly fall behind. Keeping up is easier than catching up and if you keep up, you can usually find a way to forge ahead.

Yes, you are so busy right now that you could use 48 hour days but taking just about one hour per day out of the 24 that you are allotted and only $5 out of every hundred dollars that you earn and investing that time and money in yourself can increase your future earnings a hundred fold.

There are newsletters, webinars, Tele-seminars and real brick and mortar seminars that can provide information and cause your knowledge to grow and expand so that your business can also grow and expand but you

must be willing to invest in yourself so that you can take advantage of this information…learn it…and apply it to your own internet business.

Live An Action Driven Life

Did you know that people who live an action oriented life do things in a different manner? Unlike 'normal' people, they are truly passionate about what they are doing and they will do whatever it takes because they want it bad. They want it so bad that they can't sleep at night until they achieve it.

Imagine that you are a teenage boy or a girl. You have met your first love and you want him or her so bad. If your mom or dad told you that you cannot leave the house, what would you do if you really want to see him or her? Would you sneak out at night? Would you climb out the window and slip away? You would do whatever it takes, right?

That's exactly the way action driven people do things!

Whether you identify with this or not, it remains a known fact that if you want to accomplish your goals real bad, you have to live the following characteristics:

- **You have to believe in what you are doing.**

No one would believe in you if you do not believe in yourself! If you don't have a firm belief in your mission, then who the heck is going to carry it out for you? They don't even know what your mission is! Like a rebellious teenager, you can't change them unless they truly want to change themselves!

- **You also have to develop a compelling desire to get things done.**

Like the example above, having a compelling desire is very important because if you don't have a compelling desire, most of the time, you will go halfway and later on, 'no way' because you will lose your drive.

You must have a plan.

- **If you do not have an effective plan, you will fail after awhile.**

Even with a strong belief and a compelling desire, you will still fall flat on your face and you will be confused because you want it so bad yet you can't get the results. A man without a plan is simply in dreamland.

- You must do whatever it takes all the way...

- You must have an iron will that is even stronger than Ironman's armor!

What will you do when you feel down? Are you going to live in defeat? With these 4 traits, you will have the strength to live an action driven life!

Keep a Check on Your Attitude

It is quite a decent idea to keep a check on your attitude regularly. Certain attitudes must be checked; noticed and rectified otherwise they become our philosophy, which is dangerous.

Let's check some common attitude problems.

Anger

Anger is an inflated view of one's self and attitude. Arrogance makes one deaf about other people's feelings, ideas or feedbacks. Arrogance is really a showcase of what we lack- genuine confidence. Genuine confidence gets you closer to other people arrogance takes you away.

Solution: God has given you three wonderful gifts- appreciation, confidence and humility. Practice them and you will go a long way.

EOE – Instant Expert On Everything

This is a person who has the answers to everything and is ready to speak about it at length (or a know-it-all). IEOEs can be difficult to train or teach. Any relationship with this person, whether a friend, co worker or spouse is quite difficult. Ignorance is what you get if you are such a person.

Solution: Try developing a sense of curiosity for the world and its operations. Learn to say "I don't know" and then find answers.

Refusal of Taking Responsibility for Your Own Actions

If you do not take responsibility of your actions then it is a moral or emotional problem. If we do not take responsibility the power of changing things is also lost. Blaming others give them the power to change things and eradicate your problem-solving abilities.

Solution: when you are in trouble ask these three questions- What can I do? What can I read or know about? Whom shall I consult for expertise?

AAMS- the All about Me Syndrome

This is simply selfishness personified. There's a big difference between self care which is caring about one's self and being selfish which is me first and to heck with the rest. Usually children have this behavior because it is natural during development. Growing up, means realizing that we are not the center of the universe.

Solution: Maintain a balance between taking care of you and noticing other people's lives and emotions.

Minimizing the Seriousness of Your Effect on Others

It is very easy to not notice what influence we are drawing up on others. If you are in any form of relationship what you do directly affects the other people around you. Not only your work but also your belief affects them.

Solution: Go back and see how others decisions have affected you. Then reflect on your actions and how they would have affected others.

Chapter 14

Destiny on Demand

> The reason we have poverty is that we have no imagination. There are a great many people accumulating what they think is vast wealth, but it's only money... they don't know how to enjoy it, because they have no imagination.
> **Alan Watts**

"What three business lessons did you learn from living on a farm and growing up at a garbage dump?"

I learned a lot about business and life from a working farm. Most of the people associated with farming are the most down-to-earth and genuine people you will ever meet. People who appreciate the simple things and share what they have.

One of the first things I learned was that the degree of your strength wasn't in your muscles, your head, but in your heart.

This lends to a well developed sense of appreciation and gratitude. Huge when you consider customer service regards in business. That is the foundation for a successful business between you and your associates.

The second lesson was the adaptation as a key to survival is everywhere on the farm among the animals, no matter the kind of animal or between species. Adaptation was key. This is also a huge force in business and a lesson for every CEO of a company.

Those that survived the worst of conditions were the ones that adapted to the changing environment, while influencing the others in their space. A great tool in business, adapting to a strategy in your company's strongest competitive advantages. Survival is the focus and adaptation is the single-most important element.

On the farm, you quickly learn who you can trust. The same can be said for business because a lot of people work their success with a front. Animals figure out quickly who is the real deal and who isn't. Based on that, I developed a system for determining your best value to yourself in a quick and productive fashion that gives you the tools to do it for yourself.

. . . Most people who think they are professional are flying blind.

Planning

You know the type...the person that wants to start a business and think he or she can just jump in feet first without guidance, a plan, or any sort of training as a business person. This is certainly a recipe for failure.

And...worst of all, what you will lose will be greater than your pride. You might lose profit if you screw up, you may be embarrassed if you screw up, but if you lose your credibility...you are royally screwed. You may never be able to recover. With that said.........

<u>You have to know some very important tricks of the trade that will lead the people to your door</u>.

Your advice will drive their money to you and you be paid because you will be giving them information they want...information you have spent a lifetime learning or experiencing.

The First Truth......*<u>Most people are afraid to be an entrepreneur!</u>*

You know there are many people who do anything to help other people but wouldn't know where to start or how to make money doing it. Some of my friends are the most generous and helpful people in the world but they have limited resources and limited time to do anything more than work many hours for their employer and rest a little only to work again.

However...every single one of these people

can manage three minutes to tell you about many subjects that consume them in their life...their passions, their fears and their troubles! In fact, if allowed to go on, they will ramble for hours!

Haven't you ever talked about the Super Bowl, last week's weather or even what the neighbors are doing? Sure you have.

<u>Can you imagine that you could have been paid **as much as $5,000** (or more) for that same thirty or forty-five minutes!</u>

. . . You Could Have...If You Knew the Secrets of the Professionals

Here is the deal, the coup de gras, the secret, the big Kahuna of secrets among professional public speakers and marketers:

<u>100% of all the products you **don't** have will not make any money"</u>

That's right, I teach people how to develop and sell a product to support their life business. I call it a Process 1-2-3. It is a simple process to help you develop your knowledge and turn it into a product. What may come with that are notoriety, fortune, authority, travel, responsibility, experience and trust.

Chapter 15

Life Clock ticking

One might think that the money value of an invention constitutes its reward to the man who loves his work. But... I continue to find my greatest pleasure, and so my reward, in the work that precedes what the world calls success.
Thomas A. Edison

In twenty years of successful business and professional business knowledge, I never made more than I could individually earn as a direct result of my labor.

(A huge mistake)

I knew I was worth more than that. I could never have taught myself the secrets that I needed to be a success.

<u>Then I discovered how to write a book and selling what I know as a profession. That's when my life changed forever.</u>

Don't put your faith in anyone that says they are professional unless they have been a success themselves. With more than 30 years of business experience and several million dollars of profit earned, I can sincerely and unconditionally state that this business is the most fun, the most profitable, and the most rewarding. Think about what you earn in a year, now. **Have you ever been paid $10,000 for a single hour's work?** If you are like most people, I'll bet not.

My Business Is My Life!
My Life Is My Business!

Mark Zupo 2010

I will tell you that the reward is absolutely the finest thing I ever received for any work I ever did before. When a client comes to you and tells you that something you said or did has changed his or her life forever, you will never be the same from that moment on.

And, to think that you got paid for it, too!

Building a Membership / Mentoring what You Know

-Coaching [This one is HOT]

Lead, Follow or Get Out of the Way!

Deliver impactful information from your life's experience.

Question? Can your education or experience in a specific area or industry be used to help other people solve their problems?

Question? Will your helping people to solve their problems bring you some satisfaction or reward?

Question? Does a market who is willing to pay for what you know exist?

Question? Can you feel satisfied taking money from people by selling what seems, to you, to be simple information? Consider that you could generate a few hundred, to many thousands, of dollars a month.

If this is something that you can conceive doing, then you have just made an important step in turning what you know into a business!

There are six basic steps to the process. Let's get started.

-The "How To" to it.

Step 1. Create an Outline

List what you know, your expertise or your passion in an outline that you could teach to clients. If your education or experience is in fundraising, list the forms of fundraising. List the timeline the coaching will require. Then list the responsibilities. Next, list the methods and pricing. You get the idea.

Step 2. Structure Your Program

Coaching is a methodical process and can be time consuming. It is very important that you form a schedule which details your availability and the length of lessons, etc. Make your schedule fit your own timeline and work with clients to adjust a cooperative meeting schedule.

a. How long will your program last?

b. What days / time will you meet?

c. Determine if you will meet one-on-one?

d. Determine if meetings will be in group settings?

e. Determine if your program will be delivered digitally or in person?

Step 3. Set the Price of Your Program

Structure your coaching program pricing to match your expertise and demand. Look around to other coaching programs and coaches to see what market rates are. We'll discuss some examples later.

Most personal authoritative coaches charge between $500 to $1,200 per hour. Experienced coaches may charge by the person or session at $2,500 up to $25,000. Note* Some of the highest priced jewelry is almost the same as lesser priced jewelry except that it comes from a "high-priced" business with an iconic name.

You could buy two identical rings, one from Walmart and one from Tiffany's. My guess is that the one from Tiffany's will cost several thousand more dollars...because it came from Tiffany's.

Step 4. Market your Program

Market your coaching program to a select audience of like-minded people. They will be easy to find once you have established yourself as a credible resource.

a. Look for problems that need solving.

b. Use what you know to help others.

c. Deliver great information and content if you expect to demand high prices.

d. Be professional and give freely. Abundance and quality are the keys here.

e. Use email and electronic delivery methods to distribute your sales material.

f. Always mention your products and services when you speak to others.

g. Use free webinars and Tele-seminars at every opportunity to pitch your products and services.

h. Write articles and make comments on other people's blogs and Twitter when applicable.

i. Distribute FREE reports and eBooks to anyone at every opportunity.

j. Contribute to forums when you can.

Step 5. Set the Delivery

Set the delivery of your coaching program in any form that works best for you. It can be in a digital webinar, in a Tele-seminar or in person at a local hotel. It can be an audio program or a video program. You can make all of these products from a single source and repurpose each for optimum delivery. We will discuss these options in more detail later on.

    a. Be a teacher, coach and mentor.

    b. Deliver what you know.

Step 6. Continue to Develop

As you present your program, reevaluate it to improve it, update it and advance it for precise timing and your best possible performance. You can lead people to success with your life's authority and experience. Survey your clients and ask what they want. Ask what they need and what they are looking for in terms of more value and worth.

    Follow those before you who are a success. The most successful businesses in the world that experience the fewest failures are those that are franchised, like McDonald's and Starbucks. Why? Because millions of dollars have been spent to work out the kinks, fix the bugs and correct the mistakes that years of business history have uncovered.

That said, it isn't necessary to buy into a franchise to be a success, but if you watch them and study their tactics and procedures, it is possible to mimic their success. To the point…there are a lot of people who have said, "If I had only known then what I know now." So now that you know what you always needed to know…why not share it for a profit?

Your Personal "ATM" Coaching Program

This is your plan for authoritative and trusted status as a coach and mentor:

1. Create a quantifiable plan for success.

    a. Set a dollar amount to achieve through your coaching sales.

    b. Set a price such as $197 a month for your book, audio, webinar, Tele-seminar, CD training program or DVD training program.

$200 x 12 months = $2,400 x 100 people = $240,000!!!!!

2. Build a subscription program for training or coaching.

a. 100 people x $97 = $9,700 / month! = $116,400/ year! And...you only have to have one month's content to start! I can show you how to start with only one month's content and then build contents for the following months during the second month!

3. Develop your product as a premium product limited to select members of an exclusive membership.

a. Digitally record a live training session, extract audio from video, etc. Sell the audio and the entire training DVD as a product. Use the audio as a free download to sell the entire package.

b. Turn your presentation into an audio / DVD/, transcription, workbook or slide presentation. Use them to teach others, or allow your mentees access to teach others.

This is also a great source for an affiliate program.

c. Imagine that you sell (via affiliates) 50 / month @ $497 = $24,850 /month x 12 = $298,200 / year. AND YOU DID NOTHING!

4. **Produce a "big-ticket" COACHING seminar series for selected students (or anyone else for that matter).**
a.   Imagine coaching on a cruise ship! Imagine coaching at a luxury hotel in Las Vegas! 50 tickets at $1,997 seminar = $99,850 / year. This is a one-time event! One night or one two-day weekend! What else can I say?

5. **Create a Coaching Program with a high-value "Executive," "Gold," "Diamond," or "Platinum" group participation.**

   a. 15 people at $2,000 / month = $30,000 / month x 12 = $360,000 / year.

As you can see, the options are endless. The rewards will come to those that have the guts to take the first step! Just imagine...even if you earned a portion of this? Even if you weren't that good? Even if you make mistakes, you will still make more money than you ever have made working for a living, and you'll have a lot more fun in the process.

-How Do I Start?

1. Offer a FREE seminar as close to home as possible so you'll have no travel and no excess fees or expenses.

2. Find a venue, a place you can have it, where you can gather at least 25 to 50 people.

3. Deliver your speech, seminar, information or resources for no less than 60 minutes.

4. Record it to audio.

5. Digitally record it on video, every part of it from the beginning to the end. Get plenty of audience interaction and reaction.

6. Be sure and make a gentle call to action throughout the presentation and at the end. It should be for a personal coaching program, either a one-on-one, group or digital offering.

You're Presentation Agenda

1. Develop you pricing first.

2. Develop your length and process.

3. Get a meeting room or auditorium.

4. Produce your marketing piece, flyer, billboard, poster, etc.

5. Get a sponsor to help with expenses for a return on his help.

6. Get the sponsor to help in distribution of your marketing materials.

7. Offer a FREE strategy session for members and attendees.

8. Use the questionnaire and poll method to close your coaching program and sell even more.

9. Turn your recorded program into a keynote speech, book and info product.

10. Repurpose everything you have into digital form.

The Possibilities

Let's talk about the possibilities of what might be generated from ONE Tele-seminar.

- Deliver a one hour / 60-minute Tele-seminar or webinar.

- Deliver a one hour / 60-minute Tele-seminar or webinar per week.

- Close only TWO sales from ONE Tele-seminar.

Do this on a part-time basis.

One sale @ $497 X 2 = $994 PER WEEK!

That's $3,976 per month!

That's $47,712 PER YEAR

Chapter 16

Get a Mentor

> "You have to teach people how to give you money"
> Mark Zupo

"Why do people need your program to succeed?"

Someone who has the desire to be an entrepreneur will stop at nothing to achieve their goals and dreams. However, few will ever realize their success without a plan, without a guide or tutor, mentor or leader. There is nothing more tedious to an entrepreneur than sitting at a desk and doing paperwork. That is the equivalent to writing a book about running a farm before you have ever worked on one.

You couldn't possibly know all the details and fine nuances of all the many facets that exist on a farm. It takes a lifetime of experience before you might even try to do it yourself. The result will ultimately be failure. Like a farm, it takes many "hands" and experienced professionals, equipment and an understanding of the land for it all to coalesce as a finely-tuned working machine. As well, there are many things that can go wrong so one need backups and checks and balances in place. Only experience can deliver that.

In my book **"Mind Your Business"** YOU are the business. I define who you are so you can share it with everyone else. You'll learn how to master your skills as an authority and credible person first, then, share it with others. You have to be obsessed with your expertise and willingness to share what you have learned long before you can be a success at the "Business of You!"

The point is you should be so obsessed with your business so much that you can't sleep at night because that's all you can think about. It should wake you up in the morning and charge you with energy to get running at it at the first opportunity.

That is your ultimate "business plan." To work what you love. If every company or corporation did that, if every person did that, if every school did that...where do you think we would be today?

That said, some questions come to mind;

√ If there was one thing about your life that you could change...what would it be?

This question comes with a bit of anticipation that when you adopt the change, you will be better off than before. This answer is also laced with the indication that when the change is adopted, it would lead to a **better life, fame, fortune, notoriety, recognition, admiration** or some other benefit that brings you to the forefront of other people's attention.

You should be warned though; this also comes with risk, ambiguous results, and undefined hazards. You will not be aware if the risk was worth the reward until after the change has been made and then it may be too late to reverse.

This is kind of like going back in time to kill someone and accidently killing someone else in the process forever changing the history that was established before you left. This is very dangerous territory.

To the point of that scenario;

> **Your motivation for success, freedom, and wealth must be genuine and natural in order not to upset the balance of YOUR history.**

The point is that you could not have profited from your life experiences before they happened, before you had time to hone your skills and become the authority, expert, or trusted resource that you are now.

The second question at hand is:

√ When you found that one thing that you would change, what would stop you from doing it?

Usually, we are held to our life history by the direction of our decisions and some opportunity. Notice I didn't say luck. I believe luck is the product of intuition, cognition, action, and opportunity. I don't believe it is just happenstance.

We have the ability to determine our course by some simple rules of intention:

- Achieve What You Believe Because You Believe You Can Achieve
- Know Thyself and Thy Business Because You ARE Your Business
- Build a Legacy, Not a Reputation. One Inheritable, the other...Despised
- Find The Message that Helps YOU Help Other People

The power of intention will be the driving force of your actions that determine your fate as a leader, an entrepreneur and a success in any endeavor in your life. Finally, this is the most important question that you will ever ask yourself again.

√ What do I know that will make me a living?

The most valuable resource you have is what you know! You have spent your lifetime learning and experiencing wisdom and knowledge that until now has been used for someone else's benefit. Until now you have given of yourself everything that has accumulated in your head that is of value to make someone else rich or to support their success.

What you may not be aware of is what you know comes from your passions, your experiences, your education and training. It is so valuable; you could have spent your entire life in absolute luxury just selling some portion of it to other people who need that information. **All you need is a way to present it to them!**

"You have to sometimes set unrealistic goals to achieve realistic results!"

Mark Zupo – 2009

So why listen to me?

Why Mark Zupo?

Because I started from the exact spot you are now!

Because I began with zero and built a thriving business!

Because I started small and grew with experience!

My success is directly attributed to my "mindset", my focus and my determination to succeed.

I NEVER quit!

- Mark Zupo 2010

So why listen to me?

- Because I started from right where you are too.

- Because I started from below zero and started a thriving business.

- Because I started small and grew with experience.

- Because my success is directly contributed to mindset and attitude.

- **Because I never quit!**

I've spent a lifetime developing my skills as a speaker and mentor to those who need a message that inspires and motivates them to success. In the years past as I grew and experienced life I seemed to always be behind the curve when opportunity knocked, until now. Not only am I a successful motivational and inspirational speaker, but I am also considered an authority in my industry. Who would have ever thought that someone would pay ME to talk!

As I struggled through life as an entrepreneur, I asked many, many professionals what I should do to earn money and they all said, "Become a Public Speaker, Document your Experience and SELL IT!"

Be a Speaker? Are you kidding? I can barely

keep the attention of my wife and kids let alone a group I have never met! …and…speak as a professional on a subject that I am experienced in? I don't think so.

With that, I have got to tell you that I am now successful…but it took forever to see any real money. Yes, I earned while I was learning and the money increased as I learned more from the best. I spent a year going to events, attending seminars and presenting myself at other speaker events just to see how they did it and to get comfortable with the atmosphere and energy.

In fact, I spent about **$10,000** over that year. Then I learned one simple item from a professional speaker about how to really earn when I speak <u>and it changed my life!</u> His secret---

<u>Find a Mentor.</u>

Until then, I lost money day after day. Let me say again, "I lost money day after day." My mentor was the kindest and most genuine person I ever met when it came to helping me become successful.

Oh yeah, He "chewed" my butt along the way but there were valuable lessons to be learned and it took absolute confidence in him for me to:

"Get Over It, Get On It and Get To It!"

Coaching: an easy way to make things happen

Why Coaching is the Way to Go in Team Management

When you hear the word "coach", what comes first into your mind? Do you picture a basketball team with a man/woman shouting out directions? Or perhaps a football team with a man/woman pacing to and fro and calling out the names of the players?

Coaching is no longer reserved to sports teams; it is now one of the key concepts in leadership and management. Why is coaching popular?

Coaching levels the playing field.

Coaching is one of the six emotional leadership styles proposed by Daniel Goleman. Moreover, it is a behavior or role that leaders enforce in the context of situational leadership. As a leadership style, coaching is used when the members of a group or team are competent and motivated, but do not have an idea of the long-term goals of an organization. This involves two levels of coaching: team and individual. Team coaching makes members work together. In a group of individuals, not everyone may have nor share the same level of competence and commitment to a goal. A group may be a mix of highly competent and moderately competent members with varying levels of commitment. These differences can cause friction among the members. The coaching leader helps the members level their expectations. Also, the coaching leader manages differing perspectives so that the common goal succeeds over personal goals and interests. In a big organization, leaders need to align the staffs' personal values and goals with that of the organization so that long-term directions can be pursued.

Coaching builds up confidence and competence.

Individual coaching is an example of situational leadership at work. It aims to mentor one-on-one building up the confidence of members by affirming good performance during regular feedbacks; and increase competence by helping the member assess his/her strengths and weaknesses towards career planning and professional development. Depending on the individual's level of competence and commitment, a leader may exercise more coaching behavior for the less-experienced members. Usually, this happens in the case of new staffs. The direct supervisor gives more defined tasks and holds regular feedbacks for the new staff, and gradually lessens the amount of coaching, directing, and supporting roles to favor delegating as competence and confidence increase.

Coaching promotes individual and team excellence.

Excellence is a product of habitual good practice. The regularity of meetings and constructive feedback is important in establishing habits. Members catch the habit of constantly assessing themselves for their strengths and areas for improvement that they themselves perceive what knowledge, skills, and attitudes they need to acquire to attain team goals. In the process, they attain individually excellence as well. An example is in the case of a musical orchestra: each member plays a different instrument. In order to achieve harmony of music from the different instrument, members will polish their part in the piece, aside from practicing as an ensemble. Consequently, they improve individually as an instrument player.

Coaching develops high commitment to common goals.

A coaching leader balances the attainment of immediate targets with long-term goals towards the vision of an organization. As mentioned earlier, with the alignment of personal goals with organizational or team goals, personal interests are kept in check. By constantly communicating the vision through formal and informal conversations, the members are inspired and motivated. Setting short-term team goals aligned with organizational goals; and making an action plan to attain these goals can help sustain the increased motivation and commitment to common goals of the members.

Coaching produces valuable leaders.

Leadership by example is important in coaching. A coaching leader loses credibility when he/she cannot practice what he/she preaches. This means that a coaching leader should be well organized, highly competent is his/her field, communicates openly and encourages feedback, and has a clear idea of the organization's vision-mission-goals. By vicarious and purposive learning, members catch the same good practices and attitudes from the coaching leader, turning them into coaching leaders themselves. If a member experiences good coaching, he/she is most likely to do the same things when entrusted with formal leadership roles.

Some words of caution though: coaching is just one of the styles of leadership. It can be done in combination with the other five emotional leadership styles depending on the profile of the emerging team. Moreover, coaching as a leadership style requires that you are physically, emotionally, and mentally fit most of the time since it involves two levels of coaching: individual and team. Your members expect you to be the last one to give up or bail out in any situation especially during times of crises. A coaching leader must be conscious that coaching entails investing time on each individual, and on the whole team. Moreover, that the responsibilities are greater since while you are coaching members, you are also developing future coaches as well.

Here is some of what you need to know:

- You need a mentor! **(An absolute must!)**
- Where to find speaking engagements!
- How to go from free to FEE!
- Captivating your audience to the edge of their seat!
- Eliminating cold calling to find clients!
- Selling your "back of the room" products (where the big money is)!
- The biggest lies in the information business!
- How to run your speaking business (yes, it's a business)!
- Hot to make your own products!
- How to be recognized as a professional, an authority!
- How to develop multiple streams of income!
- How electronic marketing is your best friend from now on!
- How to duplicate your success over and over!

You deserve to be RICH!

In the past 20 years, I've been a stand-up comic, a commercial pilot, managed four separate corporations, attained three degrees and spoken to many thousands of people.

> **Yet, what I learned about actually making money from my experience and knowledge I learned from a mentor in less than one year!**

Here's What You'll Get in the Information-Packed 7-Level Success System™

- Your *JumpStart*ActionPlan®
- A huge collection of speaker resources
- Speaker tools and techniques to guide you
- Book publishing tips
- Credibility-Building media resources
- Women and Minority business opportunities
- Products that you can sell to get you started
- The fastest income-generating methods
- A step-by-step process to establish yourself
- How to set your business sales on auto-pilot
- How to benefit from the coaching and mentoring market

There are a thousand ways to be successful and there are a million ways to make money. But…there are only so many strategies to be a successful public speaker.

The Secret Is Out

With all the hype about Internet Marketing, one

would wonder why anyone would attempt to be successful in what seems like a saturated market. Right? Wrong!

The internet is still in its infancy and there is room for phenomenal growth and innovation. We haven't even begun to explore all of the new technology that is waiting to be discovered on the world-wide web.

Just since I started working the Internet in the last three years alone we've seen unbelievable video presentations, amazingly fast communication connections, huge rises in users and surfers, massive Search Engine marketing techniques, tactics in web production and consumer-friendly methods to drive customers to your website and much more!

That's why I focused my attention on bringing the technology to you. That's why I am dedicated to easier understanding of the procedures and practices that give us the edge on success.

You don't need a degree in Internet Mastery but you do need some guidance from Internet-savvy educators that know the ins and outs of what to stay away from and what to be a part of. I learned all this from many years of Internet business wisdom.

And Best Of All

You can do this all from the comfort of your own

home. Imagine that. An income driving profession right from your home. Everybody's ultimate dream!

The truth is, you will learn to be self sufficient, independent, and best of all you don't have to answer to anyone! Once you are in business for yourself in a fantastic and rewarding profession, your social life will skyrocket, your identity will increase a hundred fold and you can say, "No" or "Yes "to anyone you please to.

Business requires work, it requires attention, and it requires dedication. If you think you will just get up tomorrow and be a millionaire, no one can promise you that. Look elsewhere. This is not a get-rich-quick program, system or method. It requires diligence and dedication, persistence and training. Did I say training? Yes, training.

There are a few secrets and tips that will help move you faster than someone trying this without a mentor.

> **The real secret is that you can use your spare time to create and market your own products to the vast community of interested buyers...**
>
> **by yourself!**

You don't have to be in a suit to do that. You don't have to have a hundred employees to do that. You don't have to report to a swanky office every day to do that. You don't have to fight snarling traffic every day to do that. You can do it in your easy chair in shorts and a t-shirt if you want to....even if it is 2:00 in the morning.

Generate Profits Next Week!

You could actually make profits in about a week or so, depending on how much time you have to spare, by making an informational product and posting it for sale as soon as you're done. Then, after you've perfected your technique, you can put the system on auto-pilot.

Just do it over and over again. And, you will once you've gotten your first check or made your first deposit. <u>That's what rich people do, they find the way to make money and then do it over and over again.</u>

"So what will I sell you ask?" That's easy. You have more knowledge and experience than you think and it is profitable. You just haven't learned how to sell it yet.

You study at your own pace but as guided by my materials to keep on schedule. I will schedule phone and email consultations to verify your schedule and progression. I am your resource to answer your questions.

Look, let's face it. Anyone starting their venture will be rejected from time to time. My mentor used to say, "The sale doesn't begin until the customer says, "No"". Sometimes, the customer will say,

"No". So you move on to the next customer. You adjust your product a little to make it more saleable, more attractive.

> **With the right materials and proper training you can avoid failure by following directions and trail others successes.**

You can succeed and you can get the results that you want faster than you think.

Mark Zupo

*"Rocks need polishing to become gems.
Gems need polishing regularly
to remain brilliant."*

Mark Zupo - 2009

Your Call to Action

Write, Publish and Sell Your Life Story

Turning Your Lifelong Experience into Lifelong Income

What does each of the following categories have in common? (Expert, Authority, Servant-Leader, Author, Speaker, Coach, Seminar Leader, Online Marketer)

Each is a vehicle for you to capitalize on your experience and knowledge. Each is best expressed in a manner that most everyone can understand…**in writing**. The most effective vehicle for delivering your experience and knowledge is a book. A book is a tried and true, trusted vehicle that is accepted by everyone.

Being a published author serves to spread the word about you and your gifts. It adds instant credibility and trust. There has never been a better business card than a book written by you. There is nothing that establishes authority like authorship and nothing that establishes credibility like a speaker. The more interesting consideration is you can also capture the recognition and advantages that come from speaking when you extend the reach of your message through writing. A book will help establish you as a recognized expert in your field.

The foundation for your recognition and success is in a book and a speech. It comes from an honest account of your life experiences, education and knowledge. **You have experiences and knowledge worth a fortune!**

There isn't anyone who doesn't have a story worth telling. Will you deliver a message that will improve people's lives, change their lives and empower them to action?

Questions to ask yourself:

Do you have a passion that you can share?

1. What excites you?
2. What would other people like to know about you?
3. How would someone's life be changed by your message?
4. Can you accept earning a good living sharing your message?

Would you like to write a book?

1. Is there a book waiting to pour out of you?
2. Have you ever tried to write your thoughts down?
3. Have you ever studied how to write a book?
4. Do you know how a book can help you?

Would you like to be a speaker?

1. Have you ever made a presentation to a group?
2. Could you present to people in your industry?
3. Are there people anxious to know how you can help them?
4. Has anyone asked to hear your story?

The one thing I learned long ago is that to be as good as the experts is to learn directly from the people who have done what I want to do. There is no need to reinvent the wheel. That's why I started **The Mind Your Business™ Seminars to help others find their expertise and develop their own successes.**

The 7 Level Success™ Seminars will teach you how to present your message and find the right path for reaching your audience. You will have the tools you need to establish a personal message brand and to generate income from your message.

Starting with how to distinguish yourself in the marketplace, you'll learn how to demonstrate your uniqueness, how to create additional income by learning how to write your own book and how to deliver highly effective presentations of your message.

Our expert workshop is designed to help you:

- Become a speaker to promote yourself, your products and your services.
- Build a loyal database of ideal clients and followers.
- Become an author and an authority in your industry or niche.
- Perfect the process to turn your passion into profits.
- Build an online presence and develop the "Product You."
- Build immediate income to fund your projects and lifestyle.

I've had the privilege of helping many people just like you to cash in on their message and to establish their expert status as a sought-after authority.

This is the best and most exciting time in the history of the economic world. A new breed of information-entrepreneurs is using the vehicles of social networking, audio and video technologies, print media and other offline methods to build massive productions for their life's purpose and passion .

7 Level Success Seminars™ gives you field-tested techniques for establishing yourself as an expert using your book idea and speaking abilities to open up opportunities to share your message.

Here's what you will learn about your book:
- How to find a title, subject and niche for your book
- Secret methods for creating a book in a few short days
- Self-Publishing tips to ensure maximum control and distribution of your book to information-hungry buyers
- Techniques for getting your book in front of the right people at the right time for the right price

- Methods for repurposing your book and expanding your brand
- Promotion techniques to leverage your maximum return

Here is what you'll learn about speaking:
- How to create the Seminar Checklist that ensures your success
- The greatest topic and title that drives in readers and followers
- The best days and times to book a speaking gig or seminar
- How to deliver a totally awesome presentation that kicks BUTT
- What visual methods and presentation aids work
- How to instantly create product from your live presentations

The **7-Level Success™** live event is a Super Weekend Workshop jammed with the information necessary to catapult your speaking and writing career into orbit.

The **7-Level Success™** training resources are available so that after attending a live event, you can continue to learn in the comfort of your home or office. Everyone has an individual learning style that fits. We appreciate your preferred learning style and the time you can commit, so we have the content and

experts to help you through our
7-Level Success Mentorship Program™
to help you become the in-demand expert in your niche.

The **7-Level Success Mentorship Program™** is delivered as a monthly webinar, seminar, Tele-seminar or audio program that delivers all the necessary information you will need as you need it. It is a step-by-step process to ensure that you master each step to make the next step a success.

You owe it to yourself to have every chance to make your success happen. Great **opportunities** for entrepreneurs exist right now and have never been better. There is no excuse not to take advantage of the opportunities that lie ahead of you to achieve the success you've been dreaming about.

There are two important differences between motivation and inspiration. It will become important to learn what they are and many more insightful reasons that will lead you to your success. I will teach you to understand why;

- You are the Master of Your Success
- You are the Master of Your Achievements
- You are the Master of Wealth, Freedom and Happiness

You clearly have a burning desire and driving passion to learn how to be a part of this. Passion is not enough to find success, however. Many people have this passion but few people are able to back up their passion with a quality that many people fail at – and that is TAKING ACTION.

The point of this eBook is to propel you into the correct mindset to be comfortable enough with your abilities to take action. Then you can achieve success.

I believe there are only three types of people:

The type of person who watches things happen

The type of person who makes things happen

The type of person who asks, "What happened?"

Which are you?

I teach you how to dispel the myths of Failure, Lack of Control, and Negative Influences of Other People. How to find your "Real Dream System" to empower you with the strength and desire to "Be All You Can Be" and "All You Want To Be!" If it's been done before, then You can do it, too! Be The First To Imagine It, And then...Achieve What You Can Believe!

Here, you will learn two simple goal setting methods you can do before you are done brushing your teeth in the morning.

1. How you can visualize your dreams and make them a reality.
2. How you can do anything, be anything and achieve anything that anyone else can.

"Oh really?" you say.

"Yes, really!" If it has been done before, someone just like you did it. So what makes you think you can't do it?

"They had money, they had time, they had help, they had…."

Who cares what they had! You have the same resources and they are within your reach. All you have to do is ask for it.

When it comes to life and business, it is no coincidence that some people always seem to fail while others always seem to flourish.

For sure, chance plays a role in everything. But as individuals, as business-owners, as thinkers, and as parents, we have a significant degree of control over our lives.

We can use the control we have to influence outcomes in bad ways or we can use it to influence outcomes in our favor; and in the favor of those we care about most.

When we use it poorly or when we don't use it at all, it should come as no surprise that our outcomes are bad. And when we use it thoughtfully and carefully, it should similarly be less surprising when we succeed.

Let me give you an example. At work, your employer considers you for a promotion; however, at the same time, he or she also considers several of your co-workers for a promotion, too.

Now, as many do, you might immediately say, "There's nothing I can do to influence my boss in my favor. Instead, this decision will be determined by things that are out of my control."

And, of course, when the day comes, you will not get that promotion.
Instead, someone who pushed hard to demonstrate his worthiness for the position will get the job.

And you will be left wondering why that person is always successful and always gets promotions, raises, and the adoration of management.

You might even feel resentment towards that person, even though you consider him a friend. When it comes down to it, though, it wasn't your friend who caused you to miss the promotion (or at least not to give yourself the best shot at getting it). Rather, it was your own behavior that prevented your boss from seriously considering you as a candidate.

Fortunately for you, my book, "Mind Your Business" is all about situations just like the one we described above. It's about feeling powerless when you're not; experiencing bad outcomes when there's no reason to; and finally, it's about making sure this problem stops.

Most importantly, "Mind Your Business" is about success. It is about extracting the characteristics of others that make them successful at work, in parenthood, or in the workplace; and then adopting those characteristics for your own use.

Don't stop now!

Most people do not even get this far! Now it's time for you to

TAKE ACTION!

Here is EXACTLY what to do next – Get your STEP-BY-STEP nuts and bolts crucial guide to actually start making money from your life experience, your passion and your knowledge.

I know this eBook has fired up the beast inside you, and started you thinking.

The very fact you requested this information says you have the capacity to...

Create Your Own Wealth.

"The greatest manifestation of productive effort is celebrated at the Bank!"

Unknown

So, take the plunge. Today, you will stop telling yourself you have no control over your life; and today, you will learn exactly what it means to take that control and use it to achieve success in all areas of your personal life business.

Set a goal, make a plan and DO IT!

To Your Success,

Mark Zupo

Mark Zupo

7-Level Success Mentorship Program™ Seminars

www.MarkZupo.com

You deserve to be RICH!

"Make Your Business Your Life and Make Your Life Your Business!"

Mark Zupo

"My life is changed forever now!" Yours can be too!"

I've just returned from flying my NEW Airplane!! It is a beautiful Cessna 172 with all the bells and whistles. I can't believe that I was finally able to buy it with income that I earned as a speaker and Internet Marketer. Who would have ever thought that someone would pay ME to talk!

. . . but, I asked many, many professionals what I should do to earn money on the Internet and they all said, "become a Public Speaker." Be a Speaker? Are you kidding? I can barely keep the attention of my wife and kids let alone a group that I have never met! ...and...speak as a professional on a subject that I am experienced in? I don't think so.

With that, I have got to tell you that I am now successful...but it took forever to see any real money. Yes, I earned while I was learning and the money increased as I learned more from the best. I spent a year going to events, attending seminars and presenting myself at other speaker events just to see how they did it and to get comfortable with the atmosphere and energy.

In fact, I spent about 10-thousand dollars over that year. Then I learned a simple item from a professional speaker about how to really earn when I speak <u>and it changed my life!</u>

His secret--- find a Mentor. Until then, I lost money day after day. Let me say that again, "I lost money day after day." My mentor was the kindest and most genuine person I ever met when it came to helping me become successful. Oh yeah, He "chewed" my butt along the way but there were valuable lessons to be learned and it took absolute confidence in him for me to **"Get Over It, Get On It and Get To It!"** Hey, that's my new Motto. I liked it so much that I just had the phrase Trade Marked!

. . . It is really sad... but. . .

Most of the people that try to become professional speakers lose their shirt and some more. Mostly because they don't listen. They don't follow success.

More........

They don't copy success. They don't have a mentor. Proper training and guidance is an absolutely necessary evil.

<u>This could be the day that your life changes!</u>

Simply put, with right help and direction, you can use public speaking to start you first Internet-Based Business or promote your existing business enterprises. If your speaking ability is poor then you need training. If it is good then you need training.

What did I say? <u>Right, you need training.</u> You see, being a paid armature or professional speaker will make you money BUT being a professional speaker that sells their own products will then be Highly Paid!

. . . Most speakers lose more than they earn

When speakers promote their seminar and speak for profit, they lose more than they earn! That's right. One simple tool and technique that I learned from a mentor is worth a Million dollars by itself.

. . . Professionals know the trick and tips that rake in the money!

You can too.

The first thing that you must understand is that you have to treat this like a business. If you want to stand out in this business, and you must practice the skills that make you a professional. If you don't treat it like a business and dedicate yourself to learning all the things you need to know to be successful, you will certainly fail.

More........

Many companies and many people put on public and private seminars to promote or educate other people in their company about the goods and services that they sell or to discuss the companies, losses and profits.

For the most part, they may be professionals in their field, an expert in their business, but they are certainly not professional speakers. And their wallets show it too.

. . . Most people who think they are professional are flying blind.

You know the type. The guy or gal that gives a talk at your church or Toastmasters club meeting, a family event or sales seminar for their company but....a speech that is in a safe environment. Among friends and associates. Not the type of presentation where people will "eat your lunch" if you screw up.

And...worst of all, at an event where you will lose money before you have earned it! A promoter's job may be at risk if you screw up. You company might lose profit if you screw up. You may be embarrassed if you screw up. With that said.........

<u>You have to know some very important behavior and a few tricks that will lead the people to your door</u>. Advice that will drive their money to you and be gladly paid because you will be giving them information that they want!

The First Truth......

Most people are afraid to talk in public!

You know that there are many people that would do anything to help other people. I know many friends that are the most generous and helpful people in the world. But...they have limited resources and limited time to do anything more than help them.

More......

Yet, every one of them can find a minute to two to talk about many different subjects that consumes more than thirty minutes or even an hour.

Haven't you ever talked about the Monday-night football game, last weeks' church sermon or even what the neighbors are doing? You bet you have. Could you imagine that you could have been paid as much as $5,000 (or more) for that same thirty or forty-five minutes!

. . . You Could Have...If You Knew the Secrets of the Professionals

Here is the deal, the coup de gras, the secret,

the big Kahuna of secrets among professional public speakers; "if you don't have a product to sell you haven't got anything! That's right, I teach people how to develop and sell a product to support their public speaking.

And....it's easier than you think. Think you can't do it? You sent for this information because you think that you can. I'm convinced that you can if you want to.

My job number 1 is to get you the information that you need to be successful. The secrets, the foundation for all you'll do as a public speaker.

Many business techniques that would blow away the finest MBA's from the most prestigious universities. They teach that business is tough. They teach that you have to be special to be a businessperson. **"They teach a formula for FAILURE! in the true business world."**

My job number 2 is to tell you the biggest secrets that are worth a fortune and you won't find in any university textbook. My job is to tell you what topics are the best sellers. The ones that will make you a sought after speaker and drive the kind of income you deserve.

What You Have to Learn the most effective topics and procedures that will make you an effective, energetic and high-impact speaker.

More......

There are many benefits to being a public speaker. <u>Some unbelievable benefits.</u> One that I really like is travel. I love to travel. I love to cruise to Alaska, Europe, the Mediterranean Sea, Italy, Greece, Japan, China, and New Zealand!

My wife and I just returned from New Zealand. We flew first class, (the only way I fly now), to Queenstown, (on the southern island). It was the most spectacular trip of our lifetime. Guess what---- it was hosted in the New Zealand. The total cost was over $10,000 dollars!

The speaking event paid $10,000 dollars for one hour and made over $9,000 in product sales!! **"That's right, a total of $19,000 dollars for a "working" vacation."** We stayed another ten days and visited every place you can think of on both islands. Can you believe it?

Thin you can handle that? I'll bet you could get used to being treated like a king. Some of the benefits of public speaking are remarkable. <u>I could not have been so successful without the necessary training and information in advance of trying it out on my own.</u> You must know what to do before you start out on your own.

Knowing what to do when is the key to your success. You have to be prepared for the worst before it happens to be successful in order to sound and become a visible professional.

What to do when,

- You're position is changed from the first speaker to the last speaker!
- Your scheduled time is cut in half!
- The microphone stops working in the middle of an important point!
- You are scheduled before the big "game" and the audience is anxious to get going!

And so the list goes on, which says that there are many more things to know. Ok, so it sounds simple, right? I can tell you that there is no worse feeling than standing in front of a group of people and you have forgotten your lines, forgotten your program or failed to connect with the audience on every level.

More……

Without the foundation of knowledge that is required you might be embarrassed and never move on to earning the "big" money. Don't despair, <u>a few simple techniques and a few simple tricks-of-the-trades will help you identify the problem areas and prepare you for a successful event.</u>

I have spoken for many groups of professionals who sat there and seemed to say. "Go ahead…just try not to screw up, I'll catch you." People who seemed to actually look for my mistakes so they could somehow feel superior. But… <u>with the right information, the right training and strategies, the practiced skills, you can avoid embarrassment and failure.</u> I'll help you discover the tools you need to charge ahead of the competition. It is my challenge to see you be successful as a professional speaker.

Here are some of what you need to know:

- Why you need a mentor!
- Where to find speaking engagements!
- How to go from free to FEE!
- Captivating your audience to the edge of their seat!
- Eliminating cold calling to find clients!
- Selling your "back of the room" products (where the big money is)!
- The biggest lies in the speaking profession!
- How to run your speaking business (yes, it's a business)!
- Hot to make your own products!
- How to be recognized as a professional!
- How to pick the hottest topic to speak about!
- How electronic marketing is your best friend from now on!
- How to duplicate your success over and over
- The things that you must never learn that promote failure

More......

In the past 20 years, I've been a stand-up comic, a commercial pilot, managed 4 separate corporations, attained four degrees and spoken to many thousand people.

Yet, what I learned about profitable public speaking I learned from a mentor in less than one year!

In twenty years of successful business and professional business knowledge, I never made more than I could individually earn as a direct result of my labor. I knew I was worth more than that. I could never have taught myself the secrets that I needed to be a success.

<u>Then I discovered public speaking as a profession. That's when my life changed forever.</u>

Don't put your faith in anyone that says they are professional unless they have been a success themselves.

With more than 30 years of business experience and several million dollars of profit earned, I can sincerely and unconditionally state that this business is the most fun, the most profitable and the most rewarding. Think about what you earn in a year now. **Have you ever been paid $10,000 for a single hours work?** If you are like most people, I'll bet not.

This Business Is My Life!

I will tell you that the reward is absolutely the finest thing that I ever received for any work I ever did before.

When a client comes to you and tells you that something that you said or did has changed their life forever, you will never be the same from that moment on.

And to think that you got paid for it too

More......

. . . I Have to Tell You About My Life up to Now

I grew up on a farm in Pennsylvania, about 13 miles from the nearest town with a grocery store, barber shop or movie theater. My first job was in a steel mill working to change the bricks in a blast furnace that made steel.

I had to wear a fire-retardant suit because the bricks that were damaged by the last firing had to be removed...before they cooled down. The temperature was nearly 400° degrees when I went in. The mill demanded that I do this because time was money.

This job paid a whopping $1.90 an hour! **Worse than slave labor if you ask me. And I did it gladly because I didn't know any better.**

I saw a man crushed under a steel plate. I saw my friend burned beyond recognition working right next to me. I saw many accidents and incidents that changed men's lives forever; None of them for the better. I knew that this was not the life for me.

Now I know better because I have been mentored by other people on the secrets of earning more, a whole lot more.

I was taught how to succeed, what to succeed in, how I could find my own skills and expertise to speak on. <u>My advice was to find a mentor, find a mentor, and find a mentor!</u> <u>When I did, the whole world opened up to me. I found my niche and now I am paid what I think I am worth, my real value.</u>

. . . The Benefits of the Perfect Business

There are many perks to this business. There are many social benefits, many monetary benefits and many rewarding benefits to this business. There are travel perks, social events, food, and of course, income.

More......

I have been on more than 100 cruises. More than half of them were completely free. Speaking has its benefits.

You Can Work This Business From Your Home

No special office or employees are required. No deadlines to report to work every day. No boss to argue with.

Imagine that you get a call to speak for a local group for a few minutes, maybe an hour and be paid handsomely for it. You could accept from $1,500 for the average speaking event to locals up to $10,000 for the same time for a much larger group.

Then you sell them your products after the speech and really rake it in. <u>It is not impossible to make $5,000 a week for a few minutes work.</u> Can you handle that? I'll bet you can.

<u>Most cruise lines use "enrichment speakers" for a few hours work and the cruise fees are traded for your time.</u> Imagine that, being boarded in the finest stateroom like a celebrity for a few hours of work.

. . . Did You know That…?

The majority of the income from public speaking doesn't come from the standing ovation at the end of your speech and the fame you get doesn't pay a dime? Did you know that most of the really "big" money comes from educational materials? Your materials? Once established, the educational products will sell forever and earn while your sleep!

<u>There are days that you say to yourself, "if I had only known then what I know now". Absolutely, knowledge is paramount when you get it in time, timing is everything.</u>

More...

To start, you need to cut your teeth in smaller venues like your church, Toastmasters club events and other civic associations. There is still money to be earned there as well as the "big" events in a stadium or grand hotel ballroom. Those will come too. You can be the expert putting your own public seminar on.

. . . When You Work for Someone Else

They determine what food you can afford to eat, what car you can afford to drive, what house you can afford to live in based on the money that they think you are worth! Let me say that again...<u>what they think you are worth.</u> Not what you think you are worth. It is up to you to determine your value! Not someone else.

Don't Be Surprised!

When people or groups hire you to speak they might shower you with gifts and prizes, vacations, invitations event tickets and many more things as their way of thanking you for your well prepared and well delivered speech. They will admire you for your ability to move people to action, because you can motivate them, inform them and inspire them.

. . . <u>Gee, you might even be asked for your autograph!</u>

I am still in amazement that people would want my autograph. Little 'ole me. The kid from the farm. It's true. And I gladly give it when asked. You can meet some every interesting people across this country and other countries as well. Did I mention that too? You might be asked to speak in other countries around the world too!

Imagine that your trip to Great Britain or Ireland, New Zealand or China was paid for when you are asked to speak for just an hour! Seems unimaginable but it could happen. Your social life will never be the same again.

. . . **How and Where to Start**

"Build it and they will come." Sounds "korny" but there is a ring of truth to it for sure. However, it is simple enough when you know the tricks and tips.

First, you have to be visible and recognized for your abilities and that you are open for business. I have the tips for getting started that are essential for someone to ask you to speak and build their trust in you. It can be frustrating to determine if they fit the necessary criteria for you to speak.

Do they have the money and is it available when you want it? Do they have the need for your skills and topics? Have they read about you and determined that you are the one for their cause? Have you qualified them before calling on them for more information? Are you available when they need you?

In the beginning, there are a great many actions to take before the event ever takes place. It can be frustrating. Once you have established that you are a professional, then, the people who seek you out expect to see and hear a professional.

. . . What You Won't Do

You won't cold call. A professional doesn't knock on doors, at least not in the standard way. <u>You want to establish a celebrity status and famous people don't knock on doors!</u> You want people to knock on your door. You want people to recognize you as a professional, a celebrity, a professional-level speaker, an industry expert and authority qualified to speak on the subject of your choice.

Your job is to be recognized everywhere and to put your name and professionalism where everyone can see it. You want people to hear about you, to call you and ask for more information about you, to inquire about your expertise and maybe hire you directly.

Let's talk about what professional speakers can earn. Let's talk about what the industry standard pay is and what you can command. Let's talk about the fact that this is not a get-rich-quick scheme. It requires some work, diligence and effort.

Many people in every industry has earned great incomes speaking, selling their educational and informational materials.

You can sell via TeleSeminars as well as live events. You can deliver "income driving" information via Webinars. You can give high-impact valuable information via Blogs and eZines and charge a fee for each product or service.

. . . What you want to avoid is failure of any kind.

It has been determined that 8 out of 10 people who work for a living have considered starting their own business from home.

<u>This is huge!</u> The reason most only dream about it is because they don't know where to start. Because they are afraid of failure.

When I first wanted to become a pilot, I was told that there would be years of training and examination. Re-training and more training. The funniest thing about it was I was afraid to fly!

That was OK, because I wanted so badly that

I could taste it. I knew that if I had a good mentor that he or she would teach me not to be afraid.

So I trained, and trained, and trained and practiced, practiced and practiced and eventually became a commercial pilot. One of the best and in an elite group of comrades. As a result of my success I learned how to teach flying. That's when I really got good at it. <u>Then I learned the most important secret about flying. People aren't afraid to fly, they are afraid to crash!</u>

The same holds true about public speaking. People aren't afraid to speak, they're afraid to fail at speaking.

So, in order not to fail it is important that you train, that you practice, that you get a mentor, that you seek guidance of a mentor with experience and that you see other people speak.

<u>What was really important was that all of the business experience, the industry experience and life experience I had gained up to that point helped to make me ready for the responsibility and confidence that I needed to be successful</u>. My motivator was the money without question. My first step was to learn what speakers could earn and that was enough for me.

You can earn in an hour more than most of the people that you know earn in three months of hard work for someone else. I don't want to completely focus on the money, even though it can be super but, that's what it's all about right?

Without it life is a bit more complicated, with its life can be great fun and rewarding to all those around you. It goes without saying.

There are many speakers' bureaus around the world as well as many related national associations. So you might ask if the market is saturated. Let me convince you that…it isn't. You must stand as an authority and professional to be demanded and sought after to earn the kind of sums that I mentioned before. This is big!

I mentioned earlier that I have three degrees. Well, it is the truth but that isn't what made me successful. I didn't even start college until I was 44!

I always want to get my degree but didn't have the money, didn't have the time, didn't have the determination, didn't have the confidence and didn't, didn't, didn't and a bunch more excuses. The reality was that I didn't want real success.

Mostly because I didn't know where to start. That's why I named my mentoring program, "The Learn and Earn System." You must learn in order to earn. Then why not learn from the best and brightest?

I can tell you that flight training was unbelievably expensive and the return on my investment wasn't in money but reward and the confidence of accomplishment. As I live and breathe, I also learned that it should have been about the money too to add value to the effort. I learned a lot about myself.

. . . What Will It Really Cost

It will take an investment of shorter time than it took to learn to fly. This can be accomplished in just a few weeks of the right training and guidance. When you have found the right information delivered by the right mentor, then you have a reliable method to help you succeed.

Don't forget, you are the one that has to do it though. No one can be on stage with you to hold your hand. No one will be holding cue cards or turn the pages for you.

<u>Anyone can be successful at this with the right guidance and superior information boiled down from many years of experience.</u> This alone will save you thousands of dollars that you will lose because you will never earn it!

Even a typical speaker can do this with the right

direction from trustworthy people and at a fair price. My initial assault at speaking was semi-successful and gave me the confidence to blast forward. And ...I got paid for it. I couldn't believe it. They actually paid me for talking to this small group of 45 people about "The Fear of Flying."

My first public speaking event paid almost $1,500 dollars! I never earned $1,500 flying or teaching for an hour in my entire aviation career!

In fact, it generally took three weeks of work to earn that much.

When I started flying I earned $100 a flight. It could be a 30 minute flight or a three hour flight. Both of which took all day and sometimes two days of my time and included what I paid for meals etc. Sometimes I actually lost money!

. . . Never Let It Happen

The thing that you want to never let happen is to lose money by wasting it up front. You know, before you start. So, with that said, you don't need to invest in very expensive training. Most or all of the information can be found in the advice from those who have been successful themselves.

<u>Only the best qualified and experienced people can mentor to you and give you the information that you need. Well, like me. The information I market is critical to your education.</u>

Some things that you need to know are not only how to speak but how to market yourself. This is critical to your success. You've heard the phrase about real estate, "location, location, location"?

No college ever taught me what I needed to know to succeed. What I learned was history. What I learned was how to think, how to evaluate and how to make decisions. What they didn't teach me was the formula, the path, the direction and the experience I needed up front. Yes, I am smarter because of it but it was a $150,000 dollar lesson in failure. Just because you're goo doesn't mean you will be successful. Good isn't good enough.

. . . **You don't need a degree to do this**

<u>You need guidance and direction. You need the right information. That is worth $1 Million Dollars!</u> It doesn't matter what the information costs, it

matters what it is worth to you after you learn what it will do for you.

. . . This Is What I Learned At Great Expense

This is what you need to learn too:

- How to launch you speaking career
- How to earn while you learn
- How to find speaking leads
- How to establish your credibility
     (get in print)

- How to turn a mediocre message to a hot selling topic
- How to drive interest to your website
- How to pull interest to your website
- How to make your own salable products tomorrow
     (make your own CD's and DVD's)

- How to use The rule of 21
- How to use find your 3-foot radius
- How to develop your "elevator speech"

. . . The "Sources and Marketing"

- How to demand and get the fee you set
- How to find the fastest growing market today
- How to build a rock solid, self-perpetuating business

    (thing eBay and Google)

- How to turn one speaking event into several engagements
- How to develop high content information
- How to publish your book

    (learn self-publishing techniques)

- How to market yourself and your services (someone say Internet?)

. . . Establish Your Brand Credibility

- How to package you materials the inexpensive way
- How to draw demand for your products before and after the speech
- How to stand out as a speaker against the opposition

    (be a leader not a follower)

- How to find the hottest topics today
- How to determine who is the target market

- How to find your target market
    (business, corporate, college, public seminars, adult learning)
- How to determine your expertise
- How to determine your credibility
- How to maximize your exposure
- How to make clients choose you
- How to use electronic marketing to super-size your profile
- How to develop your program that hits home with a client
    (give them what they want and more)
- How to inject humor in your presentation to lighten the load
- How to create your brand, a brand that commands attention
    (think Oprah, Elvis, Ellen, Trump)
- How to engage every age group
- How to present a striking professional appearance
    (what Hollywood used to do for a star want to-be?)

- How to engage the audience so they will never forget you
- How to work up a standing ovation
- How to promote product sales forever
      (let's talk affiliate programs)

- How to develop your website to attract wild global 24/7 attention

. . . "Show Me The Money"

The one thing I am certain about is that I always want the audience to listen to every word I say. This is because every word will motivate the audience to action. The action I want is to not only deliver a message but feel comfortable with me and trust in me enough to keep coming back. This is true for my performance in person as well as from my websites.

You have to be credible, honest and trustworthy everywhere

<u>I learned more from living a life beyond reproach than from anything else. Be honest, deliver much and remain available for consultation. These are absolutes. These are the rules.</u>

- How to convert visits to your website to sales
- How to "upsell", "presell" and "post sell" your audience
- How to find the industry contacts I need
- How to ask the million-dollar question is that keeps the money flowing
- How to train someone else to do what you do (perpetual motion)

- How to get on TV and Radio to maximize your exposure
- How to find a personal mentor who cares about you
- How to be a personal mentor to inspire others to their successes
- How to be in business for yourself not by yourself
- How to eliminate the "Stinkin' Thinkin'" and motivate yourself

. . . Give More Than Is Required

- How to create educational and informational material to generate income while you sleep
- How to get paid vacations to destination around the world

- How to enlist storytelling to bring an audience to action
- How to publish articles that make you a credible source of information
- How to find the best online shopping cart system for your website
- How to establish a database of clients and prospects that bring in massive profit
- How to never miss an engagement
- How to use testimonials to support your sales efforts
- How to get others to publish articles about you to support your credibility
- How to start your own informational seminars
- How to be a mentor to another hopeful speaker
- How to pre-sell your products to clients before they ever meet you
- How to invoke the emotion of the audience to believe your message
- How to open a speech to keep the audience glued to your every word
- How to use Viral Marketing to sell your speaking career campaign

- How to separate credibility from expertise
- How to remain personally attached to your message
- How to connect with any audience
- How to own you message and be recognized for it
- How to divide achievement from fulfillment
  <u>(Donald Trump has achieve much notoriety, Tony Robbins has fulfilled many lives)</u>

. . . Separate Yourself from The Rest

- How to change your potential to performance (one is praise and the other pays)
- How to highlight the truths and delete the negatives
- How to JumpStart your speaking career starting "yesterday"
- How to deliver the 'hook" that sells every participant
- How to enable every audience to reach for their wallet or pocketbook
- How to help any student with 3-easy ways to pay for Grad school

- How to offer solutions as well as benefits
- How to change lives forever
- How to build confidence in your message
- How to learn 4-easy ways to earn while you learn
- How to use the power of "7"
- How the number 3 becomes your best friend
-

... **Unleash the power of the Internet**

- How to dominate your market
- How to be first in a new product, service or idea
- How to think yourself rich
- How to think yourself highly effective
- How to start an 8A company for minority involvement
- How to use power words that move people to action
- How to turn "setbacks to comebacks" and build trust in your products
- How to sell persistence to overcome a resistance to buy from you
- How to turn, "would I, could I, should I to, I will, I can and I do!

By now you're wondering if I can deliver. I have combined and delivered information that is the hottest and most in-demand information on the market today. Not only will I deliver what I said I would, I'll give you more too.

Because I am genuine and I care about you. <u>Your success is paramount to my success. I believe in my success because I own it, I live it and I am sincere in my right to succeed. You must be as committed too.</u>

You can't do this on your own. I want your testimony and your endorsement and your confidence and I will work very hard for that.

This isn't rocket science; it is fairly basic information with a few secret twists. I'll give you the information and techniques that determine your income earning ability. You have to use them at your best. There are no guarantees because I can't be there with you when you deliver a speech, I can't hold your hand or turn your cue cards. But I can give you the opportunity to learn the proper way of doing things.

. . . Here's What You'll Get in the

Information-Packed Learn2Earn™ System

- Your **JumpStartActionPlan®**
- A huge collection of speaker resources
- Speaker tools and techniques to guide you
- Book publishing tips
- Credibility-Building media resources
- Women and Minority business opportunities
- Products that you can sell to get you started
- The fastest income-generating methods
- A step-by-step process to establish yourself
- How to set your business sales on auto-pilot
- How to benefit from on the coaching and mentoring market

There are a thousand ways to be successful and there are a million way to make money. But...there are only so many strategies to be a successful public speaker.

. . . The Secret Is Out

With all the hype about Internet Marketing, one would wonder why anyone would attempt to be successful in what seems like a saturated market, right. Wrong! <u>The internet is still in its infancy and there is room for phenomenal growth and innovation.</u>

<u>We haven't even begun to explore all of the new technology that is waiting to be discovered on the world-wide web.</u> Just since I started working the Internet in the last three years alone we've seen unbelievable video presentations, amazingly fast communication connections, huge rises in users and surfers, massive Search Engine marketing techniques, tactics in web production and consumer-friendly methods to drive customers to your website and much more!

That's why I focused my attention on bringing the technology to you. That's why I am dedicated to easier understanding of the procedures and practices that give us the edge on success.

You don't need a degree in Internet Mastery but you do need some guidance from Internet-savvy educators that know the ins and outs of what to stay away from and what to be a part of. I learned all this from many years of Internet business wisdom. <u>Invaluable time-saving methods of reaching your target market to monetize your potential and maximize your income.</u>

. . . and Best Of All

You can do this all from the comfort of your own home. Imagine that. An income driving profession right from your home. Everybody's ultimate dream!

The truth is, you will learn to be self sufficient, independent and best of all, you don't have to answer to anyone!

<u>Once you are in business for yourself in this fantastic and rewarding profession, your social life will skyrocket, your identity will increase a hundred fold and you can say no or yes to anyone you please to.</u>

There isn't anyone out there that do this if you really want to. Yes, it requires work, it requires attention and it requires dedication. If you think you will just get up tomorrow and be a millionaire, no one can promise you that.

The real secret is that you can use your spare time to create and market your own products to the vast community of interested buyers by yourself. You don't have to be in a suit to do that. You don't have to have a hundred employees to do that. You don't have to report to a swanky office every day to do that. You don't have to fight snarling traffic every day to do that. You can do it in your easy chair in shorts and a t-shirt if you want to.

. . . Generate Profits Next Week

You could actually make profit in about a week or so, depending on how much time you have to spare, by making an informational product and posting it for sale as soon as you're done. Then, after you've perfected your technique, you can put the system on auto-pilot.

Just do it over and over again. And, you will once you've gotten your first check or made your first deposit. <u>That's what rich people do, they find the way to make money and then do it over and over again.</u> Gee, that's not very complicated is it? Think you could do that? I can and so can you.

So what will I sell? That's easy. You have more knowledge and experience than you think and it is profitable. You just haven't learned how to sell it yet.

I'll show you how to find the most profitable topics to speak on and sell that you've had in your head for a lifetime and didn't even know it. You study at your own pace but as guided by my materials to keep on schedule.

I will schedule phone and email consultations to verify your schedule and progression. I am your resource to answer your questions.

Look, let's face it. Anyone starting their venture will be rejected from time to time. My mentor used to say that, "the sale doesn't begin until the customer says, "No"". Sometimes, the customer will say, "No". So you move on to the next customer. You adjust your product a little to make it more salable, more attractive.

That's where I help you. That's what I am good at and what you'll be good at too in time. I'm sure that you know that the best lessons learned are usually the hardest lessons learned. Well, I'm here to tell you that you will stumble a little but... **With the right materials and proper training you can avoid failure by following directions and trail others successes.**

You can succeed and you can get the results that you want faster than you think. That's where I come in.

You deserve to be RICH!

Mark Zupo

Sources and Resources

"Discover The Secret To Make Your Knowledge Sell Using My Time-Tested Strategies!"

"Your life will never be the same once you know what to do, who to talk to, how to position yourself, how to attract more business, more money and more enjoyment out of life!"

You are just one step away from a dynamic and charged opportunity to JumpStart your success with *free* membership the

7-Level Success™ Series

Insider's Membership Club.

When you join the **7-Level Success™ Series Insider's Membership Club,** you'll get you own free copy of: **You Deserve to be Rich** which is jammed packed with tips to motivate and inspire you to greater success, bigger profits and a better life decisions! **Yours *FREE!***

Here is more of what you'll get:

- **7-Tips for generating more profit today!**
- **10 methods to develop multiple streams of income!**
- **3-Secrets to the newest Social Media "Cash-Cow"!**
- **My weekly eZines with valuable insider's information!**
- **Access to my "Members-only" blog**

7-Level Success™ Series

Insider's Membership Club

members also have the opportunity to learn:

- **How to market and sell what you know!**
- **Access to expert interviews with industry leaders!**
- **How to develop a recession-proof business for just pennies!**

...and much more!

Don't waste another minute.

LET'S GET STARTED!

Mark Zupo

ABOUT THE AUTHOR

Mark Zupo is an "Accomplished Entrepreneur" who has devoted his life to helping others succeed in their goals and dreams. His goal is to help you fulfill your career goals and achieve financial freedom and independence by building the successful…"Business of You!" Mark's consulting and e-Business acumen remains unequaled as a _Life-Success Authority_. Mark is a leader, entrepreneur and mentor to many.

Mark Zupo is a dynamic and insightful speaker, recognized for his empowering and motivational focus to your success. As a driven leader commanding presence, he inspires, and with a motivates, empowers his audience.

Mark Zupo has been the driving force in changing the lives of anyone within range of his voice. Mark's "3-Foot Rule" makes him one of the most sought-after speakers in his industry.

Mark's speaking career in industry spans 25 years and he has delivered more-than, 1,200 presentations. From his experiences he has authored and co-authored many books on self-development, business development techniques and marketing enterprises. Find the topic or topics that are a sure fit for you and your organization, and schedule Mark to speak at your event soon.

I have always believed that you're destiny is determined when the decisions you make are put into action. I also believe that there is a greater power that guides your decisions. Ultimately, the path your life takes is directly proportional to the amount of education you have and the amount of labor you put into it. Some of the guidance you get is a direct link to your past experiences. Put your hand in the fire and you get burned. Chances are you will remember that lesson and not repeat the exercise and get burned twice just as in real life.

Most people have a set of rules they follow based on their experiences, education, wants, needs and desires. Those that choose to follow a path that they themselves question…usually leads to an end that was predictable and distasteful. With that in mind, you should follow the leadership of those who have succeeded before you by using their experiences, failures and successes as a guide to moving on your own ventures. As an example, watch someone else get burned and you will likely not repeat their actions in fear of the results you witnessed.

However, we strive to have what our neighbor has and sometimes more even if we really don't need it. We want to be like someone we respect and admire and are willing to change our life to accommodate that desire. That said, some questions come to mind;

√ If there was one thing about your life that you could change...what would it be?

This question comes with a bit of anticipation that when you adopt the change you will be better off than before. This answer is also laced with the indication that when the change is adopted it would lead to a better life, fame, fortune, notoriety, recognition, admiration or some other benefit that brings you to the forefront of other people's attention.

You should be warned though, this also come with risk, ambiguous results and undefined hazards. You will not be aware if the risk was worth the reward until after the change has been mad and then it may be too late to reverse. Kind of like going back in time to kill someone and accidently killing someone else in the process forever changing the history that was established before you left. This is very dangerous territory. To the point of that scenario, your motivation for success, freedom and wealth must be genuine and natural in order not to upset the balance of YOUR history.

The second question at hand is:

✓ When you found that one thing that you would change, what would stop you from doing it?

Usually, we are held to our life history by the direction of our decisions and some opportunity. Notice I didn't say luck. I believe that luck is the product of intuition, cognition, action and opportunity. I don't believe it is just happenstance. With that in mind, we have the ability to determine our course by some simple rules of intention. They are that we must:

- Achieve What You Believe Because You Believe you Can Achieve
- Know Thyself...and Thy Business Because You Are Your Business
- **Build a Legacy Not a Reputation, one is Inheritable and the other is Despised**
- **Find The Message that Helps YOU Help Other People**

The power of intention will be the driving force of your actions that determine your fate as a leader, an entrepreneur and a success in any endeavor in your life. Successful people do what other people don't want to do.

To Your Success...

Conclusion

We all understand, regardless of where we are in life, no matter what business or industry we entertain, that we are in the people business. What differentiates us from the masses is that we understand that we are also in the ME business too. We have spent our entire lifetime building, educating, improving, detailing, sharpening, motivating, strengthening and training ourselves to be the finest product ever to hit the market. You have improved on the invention of YOU in every way until you have become the tool of choice in your business and industry.

The truest business YOU have ever worked in is the business of your life, and you have never been paid your real value and your real worth. It is time that you be rewarded for a lifetime of labor and attention. The product of YOU is ready and waiting to be unleashed on the world, and now is the time.

The obstacles to success are not the things we think we lack to be successful; the true obstacle is getting rid of the things that we have that get in the way of our success.

Mark Zupo

"Own your dreams and plan your success."
Mark Zupo - 2010

Sources and Resources

Mark's speaking career in industry spans 25 years. He has delivered more-than, 1,200 presentations. From his experiences he has authored and co-authored many books on self-development, business development techniques and marketing enterprises. Mark speaks on several topics that enlighten, entertain and motivate his audiences to action!

Mark's Most Requested Topics/Programs:

- **My Adversity University**

   "Build Power, Credibility and Respect from Life's Lessons"

- **Champion Your Success**

   "Achieve What You Believe, Believe What You Can Achieve'

- **7-Secrets of Business Success**

   "The Keys to Wealth and Freedom"

- **Leadership**

   "From Ability to Credibility"

Schedule Mark to Speak at Your Next Event!
Contact us: 1-678-640-0585

Mark Zupo

On-line: *www.MarkZupo.com*
markzupo@gmail.com

www.7LevelSuccess.com

Opportunity

Don't Spend Years Trying to Write Your Book!

There is a Fast and Painless Way to Write a Book without Having to Actually Write it Word for Word!

The Secrets to Writing & Selling Your First Book Fast are within reach in:

The Original How to "Write and Sell Your First Book" Workshop

You have always thought of writing a book, but you just can't find the time, right? Now you can…because I will show you how to do it faster than you ever thought possible!

The **"YourFastBook™"** Workshop will give you all the tools you'll ever need to "blast" out a book in no time flat!

In the "YourFastBook™" workshop, you'll learn:

- ➢ How to write your book without ever putting pen to paper!
- ➢ How to market your book without ever paying

a publisher!
- ➢ How to make your book available to millions with a click of a button!
- ➢ How to avoid the 10 most common mistakes authors make!
- ➢ How to protect your copyright with this simple free technique!
- ➢ How never to pay a royalty keeping all the profit for yourself!

Still Not Convinced?

I am the author or co-author of more-than 23 books to date. I am a "top-selling" author and credible authority on the self-publishing secrets that the conventional industry publishers don't want to you to know.

Check this out! When you enroll in my award-winning workshop you'll get all this and more:

- ✓ How to compose your book in one day!
- ✓ How to give your book an award-winning title!
- ✓ The three secrets to every author's success with future orders!
- ✓ How to turn your book into a "Money-Machine."
- ✓ How to make people pay five times what you paid for printing!
- ✓ How to develop multiple streams of income from your book.

You deserve to be RICH!

You MUST get in on this workshop right NOW!

Classes fill up quickly, so <u>sign-up now and become a self-published</u> <u>author</u>!

Workshop Details:

Become an author and wow your friends and relatives. Start your book now by enrolling in this exclusive workshop today!

Turn your computer into your personal "ATM".

See what other authors say about the YourFastBook™ workshop.

"Unbelievable! What could be more fun than writing a book that becomes your signature trademark? I am really proud to be a part of this seminar and see just what anyone could do with the information that they already had. Writing a book is more fun than I ever imagined. I was absolutely amazed at the speed at which I can write a book when I thought that it would take years to complete.

"I could never have imagined that I could be a

published author until I met Mark Zupo. He allowed me to think on a different level about traditional publishing. I am now a self-publishing advocate forever!"

"When I enrolled in Mark's workshop, I was skeptical and reserved to think that I had a book in me that someone would want to read. Now I know that my story is as powerful as any book that has ever been written. I am empowered as a new author to help other people write their story too."

"I've always felt I had a book within me. Years ago, I wanted to be a children's book author. I even took a well-known children's literature course I saw advertised in a magazine, and for which I paid dearly. Rejection slips kept coming back after sending in my queries to traditional publishing companies. I finally said, "To heck with this," and packed all my thoughts and papers away.

"Then, I met Mark. His enthusiasm and down-right sincerity convinced me I could create my own book. Now, I'm a published author! I would not hesitate to tell everyone to take Mark's course. Not only does he know what he's talking about, but he has the proof to back it up."

You deserve to be RICH!

Choose the One-on-One Book eConference Package with Mark Zupo

The Executive Author Conference:

- **eConference 1:** We will nail down the focus of your book, the title and niche the market wants and needs, and the idea and synopsis. Then we'll devise a plan for writing, printing, marketing and self-publishing it. We will tailor your personal objectives and timeline for completion of the book content. I will give you some of the resources for the writing, printing and publishing you will need at this stage.

- **eConference 2:** Here we will evaluate the content of your book and formulate questions and the answers that will deliver the information that will become chapters. We'll talk about the process of establishing a brand, finding a market, positioning your book for discovery and creating methods of future income from your book.

- **eConference 3:** In this session we bring together the content, the format and the completeness of the book. We discuss income streams and methods for future books. At this stage we can start to see the results of the book in real life.

Note: We will schedule three one-hour, one-on-one conferences

(via Freeconferencecall.com, iChat, Skype or telephone). Also, there will be 2-3 additional hours of discussion via email to unite your work with the industry standard for what a book must contain.

The purpose of this package is to focus your idea and material into a print-ready product to begin your life as a self-published author.

    This package is not for people who sit around and talk about how hard it is to write a book! **This package is a proven method of self-publishing.** This is your opportunity to be a self-published author with lightning speed!

SCHEDULE **YOURFASTBOOK™ Executive eConference** now!

Mark's Books:

1. **How I never climbed Mt Everest**
   And 23 other non-events that shaped my life

2. **From Mess to Millionaire**
   One Man's Story of Failure to Success

3. **Speak for Yourself**
   The 7-Secrets of How to Make your Living Speaking

4. **Dean of the DUMP!**
   Life's secrets I Learned When I lived at the Garbage Dump!

5. **Mind Your Business**
   How to Re-Package your Life Experience

6. **Leadership**
   From Ability to Credibility

7. **Achieve what You Believe**
   Finding Dynamic Success in Self-empowerment

DISCLAIMER

-- *This is the stuff that makes the lawyers happy.*

This information in this book is strictly for informational and educational purposes only. The author and/or publisher do not guarantee that anyone using any of the information, tips, techniques, etc. from this book will become successful. The author and/or publisher shall have neither liability nor responsibility to anyone with respect to any loss or damage caused, or alleged to be caused, directly or indirectly by the information contained in this book. No guarantees are made that you will achieve any results from our ideas and techniques in our material. The information presented herein represents the view of the author as of the date of publication. The author reserves the right to alter and update his opinion Any slights of people or organizations are unintentional. You should be aware of any laws which govern business transactions or other business practices in your country and state. Any reference to any person or business whether living or dead is purely coincidental. We do not purport this as a "get rich scheme." All trademarks belong to their respective owners.

The publisher has strived to be as accurate and complete as possible in the creation of this report, notwithstanding the fact that he does not warrant or represent at any time that the contents within are accurate, due to the rapidly changing nature of the business. However, there may be mistakes in typography or content. The purpose of this e-book is to educate.

While all attempts have been made to verify information provided in this publication, the publisher assumes no responsibility for errors, omissions, or contrary interpretation of the subject matter herein. Any perceived slights of specific persons, peoples, or organizations are unintentional.

This book is a common-sense guide to marketing online. In practical advice books, like in anything else in life, there are no guarantees of income made. Readers are cautioned to reply with their own judgment about their individual circumstances and to act accordingly. This book is not intended for use as a source of legal, business, accounting or financial advice. All readers are advised to seek services of competent professionals in legal, business, accounting and finance fields.

This information is presented for educational and informational purposes only and is not intended to be a substitute for professional advice. Never disregard professional advice or delay in seeking it because of something read or heard.

We make every effort to ensure that we accurately represent our products and services and their potential for income. Earning and income statements made by our company and its customers are estimates of what we think you can possibly earn. There is no guarantee that you will make the level of income you desire, and you accept the risk that the earnings and income statements differ by individual.

As with any business, your results may vary and will be based on your individual capacity, business experience, expertise, and level of desire. The testimonials and examples used are exceptional results, which do not apply to the average purchaser, and are not intended to represent or guarantee that anyone will achieve the same or similar results. Each individual's success depends on his or her background, dedication, desire and motivation.

The use of our information, products and services should be based on your own due diligence, and you hold harmless our company for any success or failure of your business that is directly or indirectly related to the purchase and use of our information, products and services.

"MAKE YOUR BUSINESS YOUR LIFE AND MAKE YOUR LIFE YOUR BUSINESS!"

- **MARK ZUPO**

Mark Zupo

You deserve to be RICH!

Mark Zupo

You deserve to be RICH!

www.ingramcontent.com/pod-product-compliance
Lightning Source LLC
Chambersburg PA
CBHW070823250426
43671CB00036B/1851